New Directions in Italian Architecture

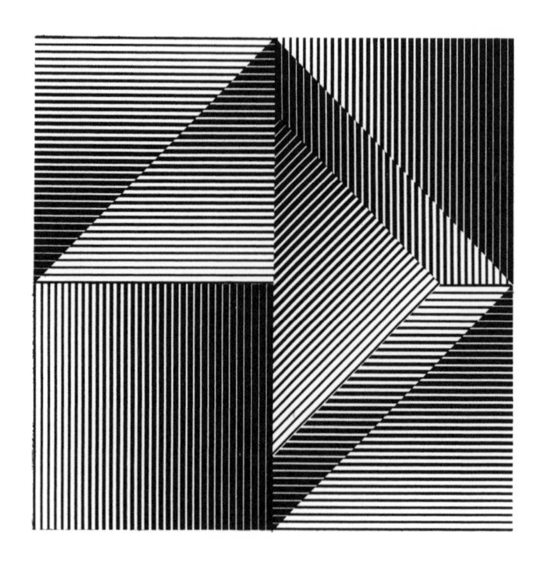

VITTORIO GREGOTTI

NEW DIRECTIONS IN ITALIAN ARCHITECTURE

GEORGE BRAZILLER NEW YORK

Translated by Giuseppina Salvadori

For information address the publisher:

George Braziller, Inc.

One Park Avenue

New York, N.Y. 10016

Library of Congress Catalog Card No.: 68–57723

Designed by Jennie Bush and Mila Macek

First Printing

Printed in U.S.A.

CONTENTS

ABBREVIATIONS

A.L.S.A.	L'Associazione Libera Studenti Architetti
A.P.A.O.	L'Associazione per l'Architettura Organica
B.B.P.R.	An association of architects Gianluigi Banfi, Lodovico Belgiojoso, Enrico Peressutti, and Ernesto M. Rogers. Known as the B.P.R. after Banfi's death.
C.I.A.M.	Congrès Internationaux d'Architecture Moderne
E.U.R.	Esposizione Universale Roma
I.L.S.E.S.	Istituto Lombardo di Studi Economici e Statistici
I.N.A.	Istituto Nazionale Assicurazioni
M.I.A.R.	Movimento Italiano per l'Architettura Razionale
M.S.A.	Movimento di Studi per l'Architettura

INTRODUCTION

This book is not a history of modern Italian architecture; neither is it a systematic survey. It might be considered an illustrated essay on Italian architecture since the Second World War, although the origins of difficulties and accomplishments have been sought in periods preceding the modern movement in Italy. In my examination of the subject as a whole, I have attempted to consider many elements, both historically and quantitatively. I have also written with the awareness that no book on the history of modern Italian architecture, not even a short book such as this one, exists as yet. The subject has been dealt with in a series of brilliant but far from comprehensive attempts at writing such a work. The present book, however, is not that of an historian, but rather of a man who has lived, as an architect, through the ups and downs of Italian architecture over the past fifteen years, and whose aim is to set forth his own preferences and the bases for them; in other words, to present as part of architecture his own ideas on the history of that architecture.

The influence on modern Italian architecture of the movements in international architecture during the last thirty years has been greater than many have wanted to admit. I will not dwell on this point, but I must say that Italian architecture has experienced this influence in various forms, albeit unconsciously. On the periphery of the changes in international culture, it has often seemed to take advantage of the experiments of the modern movement without carrying them out in a direct manner, and to have done so through some brilliant responses to separate opportunities. The brief history of modern Italian architecture is marked by a continuous succession of crises.

Rather than implying a definite change of direction, these crises were generally turning points in name only, growing out of that typical flaw of Italian culture, the search for a "way out." Yet it cannot be denied that these crises have given rise, in an often remarkably aggressive and original way, to some of the problems which have developed in contemporary society over the past fifty years.

I believe that the development of Italian architecture demonstrates some characteristics which can be useful on an international cultural level. First, it is a dialectic between architecture and the notion of history and traditions which have been a continuous inspiration to itself both on the level of architecture and urban development, and on the level of methodology and linguistics. This led frequently to solutions which were antithetical to the modern movement; the process of transformation very often led to a loss of contact with reality, or revealed profound and concrete discrepancies.

The second characteristic is a constant debate and steady interaction between ideology and language. There is an attempt, on the one hand, to make them include or grow out of each other and, on the other hand, to contrast them, giving rise to opposing solutions (often more intense and meaningful on the local than on the international level), outweighing political, technological, methodological, and socioeconomic considerations which are frequently outmoded or contradictory.

The third characteristic arises out of the first two and consists of a state of basic ambiguity, through complexity of meaning as much as through the unsuccessful solution of problems. This ambiguity forms the basis of the expressive language of the most interesting Italian architecture.

Those are the problems which we will consider in this book. An attempt will be made to discover some thread of continuity in the striving of Italian architecture toward reality, in that architecture's hitherto unsuccessful struggle to combine needs, projects, methods and realization, utopia and reality, in a single effort.

THE FORMATION OF THE MODERN MOVEMENT 1918–1943

NEARLY the whole history of the relationship between modern Italian architecture and Italian culture is linked to the Futurist movement: this included the work of architects Antonio Sant'Elia, Mario Chiattone (*Fig. 1*), and even the more peripheral work of Virgilio Marchi and Enrico Prampolini. However, if it is true that Futurism—with its glorification of the machine and its efforts toward a radical renewal of architecture—was the Italian art movement most fundamentally a part of international culture, it is also true that after the First World War modern Italian architecture was born and painfully developed in a climate which was for the most part anti-Futurist in culture and neonationalistic in politics. Futurism itself ended up by following this neonationalistic path, which led to a seemingly anti-romantic attitude toward the "realities" of Italian life, realities which were, in fact, not concrete and which were aimed in their totality at conforming with a body of myths and illusions.

The myth of the Mediterranean and the monumental tradition; the myth of the Italian genius which turned its back on the real role of Italian culture, a culture which had already been outside the mainstream for a century; the myth of a strong and hard-working people; rather than recognizing the realities of the myth of a young nation, rather than the recognition of false prosperity based on interior disorganization; the myth of a return to order which, in a substantially backward nation such as Italy was in 1920, did not imply a rational organization of resources but simply political restoration and economic privilege. All this was brought out by the defeat of the progressive forces and by the triumph of fascism in 1922, which incarnated the ideals of the small, provincial, ambitious, frustrated, and mobile Italian middle classes.

In 1919, at the end of the First World War, the Italian cultural front contained such groups as La Ronda in literature and Valori Plastici in painting, which believed that the experiments of the prewar avant-garde artists in Europe had failed, and which adopted as a result a new classicism, denying any internationalism in the formal language of the arts. Architecture, by ignoring Futurism, which was heir to the romantic "twilight" on the one hand and depended on the aesthetic of the machine, rejecting, therefore, the bourgeois social order, on the other, turned to two principles: a return to order and the rejection of eclecticism. A group of Milanese architects most representative of these principles of a return to order between 1919 and 1925 turned to these very sources and perspectives. Their original point of view was exemplified by the group of painters known as the Milanese 900, which had inherited a positive outlook toward the metaphysical painting of Giorgio de Chirico and was devoted, through classicism, to an assertion of the Italian pictorial tradition of heavy, circumscribed forms, and to a renewal through that tradition of what was most typical in the national culture.

In architecture, Giovanni Muzio was the most significant representative of this trend. In the Via Moscova apartment house of 1923 (*Fig. 2*), he experimented with a syntax consisting of a stylization of classical elements; it was an architecture suspended between metaphysics and history and deeply influenced by the current Austrian experiments, which strove toward a house without a true facade or back but rather with an architectural vocabulary of a series of interweaving fragments within a continuous and circumscribed volume.

The vocabulary to be employed in an extension of the contemporary city was consciously based on this neoclassical ideal. This element, so interesting in the urban culture of the years in which the Milanese 900 was prominent, appealed to Giuseppe Definetti, who brought back to Italy some of the revolutionary, antidecorative ideas of the Viennese architect Adolf Loos. In 1925, Definetti built La Meridiana in Milan as his manifesto (*Fig. 3*). This same classicistic approach can be discerned in the work accomplished in those years by Gio Ponti, both in architecture and in applied art, as he combined the Italian craft tradition with the work of Josef Hoffmann and the Wiener Werkstätte. As early as 1919, Giovanni Greppi had designed a building in the Via Statuto in Milan (*Fig. 4*) which was strictly derived from the Austrian Secessionsstil (Art Nouveau). The same tradition influenced Marcello Piacentini's early work in Rome, although its effects there were altogether different.

With the exception of the accomplishments of Giulio Magni, Giuseppe De Angelis, and Giovan Battista Milani at the beginning of the century, the first attempts at architectural renewal developed within a very heavy eclectic, monumental tradition, which was oriented toward the past. This academic tradition can be summed up in the personality of the historian and architectural theorist Gustavo Giovannoni. Before 1925, the renewal movement rediscovered baroque architecture, finding in it a style whose tormented, complex forms were suited to modern complexity as well as the value of a verbal architecture; it also gave rise to timid imitations of the style of the Viennese Secession. On the urban level, there was an attempt to introduce a sense of the picturesque into the city, and in 1927 Roman architects took part in a competition for the town planning of Milan. The architects of Milan, from Giuseppe Definetti to Ponti and Giovanni Muzio, formed a united front in the competition, indi-

1. *Mario Chiattone: Groups of buildings for a modern city, 1914, drawing.*

2. *Giovanni Muzio: Apartment house, Via Moscova, Milan, 1923.*

3

cating those parts of the city which best lent themselves to substantial change. This was the first introduction of scientific town planning in Italy.

Both the Milanese 900 and the Roman neobaroque movement, therefore, stemmed from a moderate avant-garde position, and for some years their adherents disputed with the rationalists the claim of renewing Italian architecture.

Historically, 1926 was the year in which Group 7 was founded and Italian rationalism was born. The writings of that movement were as moderate as those of the 900. The joint declaration of the members of Group 7—Sebastiano Larco, Guido Frette, Carlo Enrico

3. *Giuseppe Definetti: Casa della Meridiana (Sundial House), Milan, 1925.*

4. *Giovanni Greppi: Collini house, Via Statuto, Milan, 1919.*

Rava, Luigi Figini, Gino Pollini, Giuseppe Terragni, and Adalberto Libera—which appeared in 1926 in the magazine *La Rassegna Italiana*, read:

> The hallmark of the earlier avant-garde was a contrived impetus and a vain, destructive fury, mingling good and bad elements: the hallmark of today's youth is a desire for lucidity and wisdom. . . . This must be clear. . . . We do not intend to break with tradition; tradition transforms itself, and takes on new aspects beneath which only a few can recognize it. The new architecture, the true architecture, should be the result of a close association between logic and rationality. . . .

The group of heterogeneous personalities who formed Group 7 had a definitely anti-Futurist attitude; yet in Roverto (which was a frontier city up to 1918) the young Libera, Pollini, and Luciano Baldessari perceived the first indications as to the nature of modern culture and modern architecture from the Futurist Fortunato Depero: The revelation given them was Le Corbusier's book *Vers une architecture* (1927). Baldessari did not join the group, which he considered to be tainted with fascism, as a result of his experience as a stage designer in Berlin from 1922 to 1926.

In 1927, some members of Group 7 showed their work at the Werkbund Exhibition in Stuttgart. In the same year, Baldessari, back from Berlin, designed a bookstore dealing with the European avant-garde. In 1930 (in Monza, the center of the Biennale of Industrial and Decorative Arts, later to be called the Triennale), some members of Group 7, along with Piero Bottoni, built the Casa Elettrica and exhibited designs and models, among which was the Officina del Gas, one of Giuseppe Terragni's most interesting projects (*Fig. 5*). By 1929 Terragni, together with Pietro Lingeri, had already built in Como what can be considered the first work of Italian rationalism, the Novocomum apartment, in which traces of Soviet building experiments were evident (*Fig. 6*). This influence had risen out of Futurism, which had been in constant touch with the Russian avant-garde and shared with it elements of plastic dynamism and mechanical-industrial forms.

In 1928, Libera organized the first show of the M.I.A.R. (Italian Movement for Rationalist Architecture; see also List of Abbreviations) in Rome, including in it works by Group 7 architects; this show was sponsored by the Fascist Union of Architects. The situation in Rome was politically and professionally more difficult than in Milan. By 1930 the political unions had taken command, and in 1931 they condemned the second M.I.A.R. exhibition, organized in the bookstore of the art critic Pietro Maria Bardi, mainly because of his book *Rapporto sull'Architettura* (*A Report to Mussolini on Architecture*), in which, by speaking of rationalist architecture as the architecture which embodied the ideals of the fascist revolution, he had brought

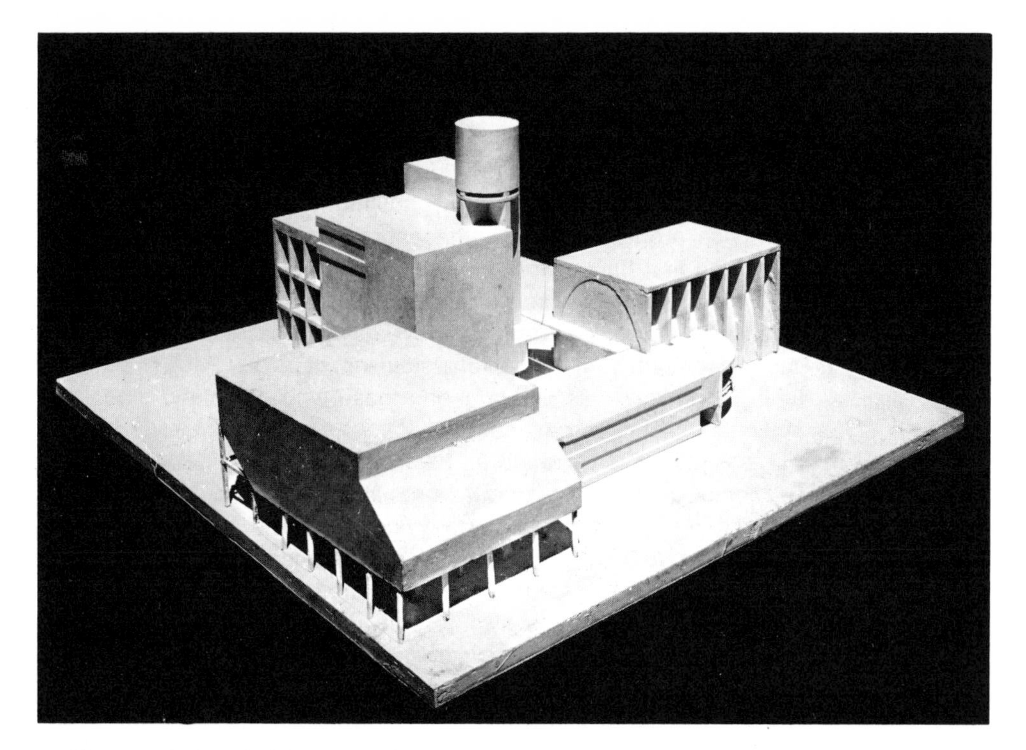

5. *Giuseppe Terragni: Officina del Gas, 1927, model.*

6. *Giuseppe Terragni: Novocomum apartment house, Como, 1929.*

7. *Edoardo Persico with Marcello Nizzoli, Giancarlo Palanti, and Lucio Fontana: Large hall, 6th Triennale, Milan, 1936.*
8. *Aldo Andreani: Palazzo Fidia, Milan, 1930.*

rationalists. At the same time it was the impetus which undoubtedly gave birth to some of the most original and committed rationalist works.

It can be said that the fight for modern architecture was carried out in three basic areas:

1) In exhibitions. The Exhibition of the Revolution in 1932 in Rome and particularly the Triennale exhibitions which, in a very representative way, epitomized the history of modern Italian architecture.

2) In competitions. The competition, announced in 1934, for the Palazzo del Littorio which was to have been the Fascist Party's headquarters in Rome, but was never built; the competition for the new towns in the Lazio region of central Italy; the competition for the Florence railroad station; and the competition for E.U.R. 42 (Esposizione Universale Roma see page 32), the large international exhibition which was to have been held in 1942 in Rome.

3) In the lively polemics carried out in specialized and nonspecialized magazines, particularly in *Casabella*, but also in newspapers and even in the Chamber of Deputies.

From 1932 to 1936, Pietro Maria Bardi and Massimo Bontempelli published the magazine *Quadrante* in Milan, as a medium through which the leftist followers of the fascist minister Bottai again attempted to impose rationalism as the official architecture of the regime. Piacentini, adopting a middle-of-the-road policy, looked for a way to reach an understanding with the rationalists by inviting Giovanni Michelucci, Gaetano Minnucci, Pietro Aschieri, Gino Capponi, and Giuseppe Pagano to work in the project for the University Precinct in Rome in 1932.

In 1932, the exhibition for the tenth anniversary of the Fascist Revolution had given rationalism a great opportunity to express itself through a vocabulary influenced to a large extent by the Milanese 900 (particularly the painter Mario Sironi) and even by Futurism. In 1933, Piacentini supported the rationalists in the competition for the Florence railroad station (*Fig. 9*), thereby working toward the success of Michelucci's group, which was thus given the opportunity to build one of the best examples of Italian architecture of the interwar period. The covered arrival corridor of the front station and the continuous external glass paneling, are formally brilliant solutions. Every government commission, however, entailed political and professional compromise and a silencing of debate. In 1934, for example, the rationalists lost the national competition for the Palazzo del Littorio.

The Triennale exhibitions, where the lines were more clearly drawn and the conflict more open, offered rationalist architects few opportunities for experimentation, oportunities which were very rare during those years, when they had to rely for the most part on private commissions. The old Monza Biennale became the Triennale in 1930 and was moved to Milan, where it was held in the new building of Giovanni Muzio; in 1933, the Triennale was still largely under the classicistic influence of the Milanese 900, but the sixth Triennale in 1936 marked a definite step toward rationalism (*Fig. 10*). Pagano built a rigorously rationalistic entrance hall; Luigi Figini, Gino Pollini, Terragni, Lodovico Belgiojoso, Enrico Peressutti, Ernesto N. Rogers, and Piero Bottoni built a series of small rationalistic dwellings in the park. In 1934 there had been an aeronautics exhibition for which Edoardo Persico and Marcello Nizzoli created the Sala delle Medaglio d'Oro (*Fig. 11*), one of the most rigorously poetic expressions of Italian rationalism. It was to exert a powerful influence

9. *Virgilio Marchi, Pier Nicolò Berardi, Italio Gamberini, Sarre Guarnieri, Leonardo Lusanna: S. M. Novella Railroad Station, Florence, 1934.*

through its spatial modularity, characteristic use of black and white, and the placement of exposed elements as if magically suspended.

After 1936 a strong antimodern reaction emerged in Italy, as well as in France, Germany, Russia, and the rest of Europe. The seventh Triennale of 1940 evidenced a shift toward the academy; the political regime by now clearly sided with the most reactionary groups.

The most important expressions of Italian rationalism date back to 1932–1936; some houses, including Figini's house in Milan (*Fig. 12*), the first building built on pilotis, and strongly influenced by Le Corbusier's Villa Savoye; the Olivetti building of Figini and Pollini (who, together with Terragni and Libera, were the only members of Group 7 to remain faithful to the principles of modern architec-

10. *Franco Albini, Ignazio Gardella, and others: Apartment for four people, 6th Triennale, Milan, 1936.*

11. *Marcello Nizzoli, Edoardo Persico: Sala delle Medaglie d'Oro, Italian Aeronautics Exhibition, Milan, 1934.*

ture); the Parker store of Persico and Nizzoli; the first aesthetic experiments of Albini and the group of Como architects (also supported by the small circle of Italian abstractionists); the works of Pietro Lingeri, Cesare Cattaneo, Gianni Mantero and, above all, Giuseppe Terragni (*Figs. 13–14*), whose Casa del Fascio, Villa Bianca, and Sant'Elia Kindergarten form the nucleus of the Italian rationalist language.

An authentic language in Italian rationalist architecture was thus established. It was related to the methodological principles of the modern movement; but clearly identifiable in quality as well as in its limiting the struggle for a modern architecture to a battle of styles. Persico wrote in *Domus* in 1934:

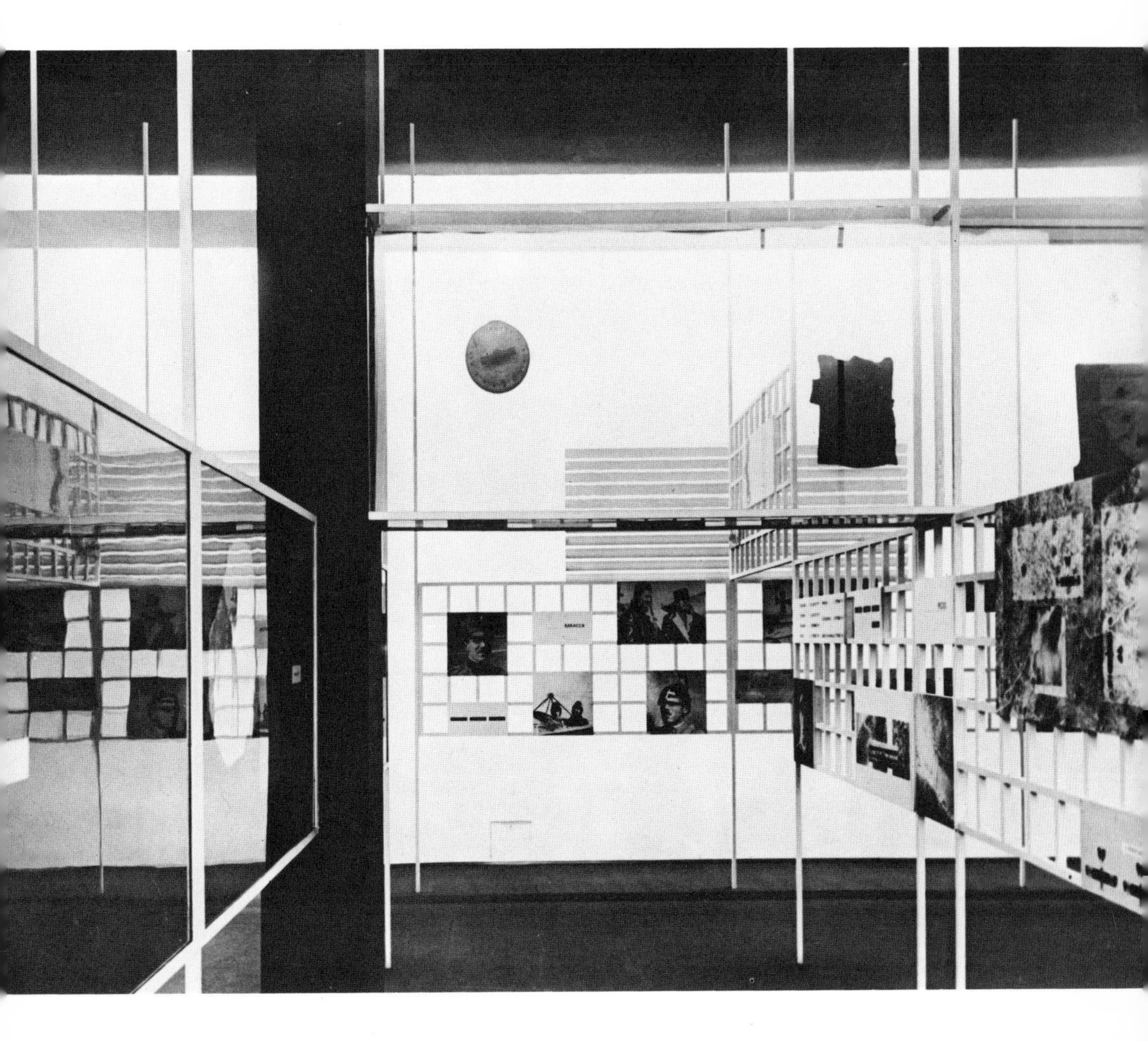

Today the artist must face the most troublesome problems of Italian life: the reliance on set theories and the will to carry to the very end the battle against the demands of an "anti-modern" majority.

Such demands, repudiated by the idealistic stubborness of Italian polemicists, constitute the heritage that we will leave to coming generations, after having fatally wasted our time with stylistic problems; the most important and pressing problem of the culture of this obscure period of world history.

Persico died suddenly in 1936; this marked the beginning of the retreat of modern architecture. In a way, 1936 is a crucial date: it marks the apex of the rationalist ideal as it was ideologically set forth

12. *Luigi Figini, Gino Pollini: House of Luigi Figini, "Journalist Village," Milan, 1934–35.*

13. *Giuseppe Terragni: Casa del Fascio, Como, 1932–36.*

14. *Giuseppe Terragni: Sant'Elia Kindergarten, Como, 1936–37.*

in *Casabella.* Before 1936, only three really interesting works had been completed in Rome: Mario Ridolfi's post office in the Nomentana district (*Fig. 15*), his apartment house in Via S. Valentino (*Fig. 16*), and the project for the Pretura Unificate (Unified Magistrate's Court) by Ludovico Quaroni and Saverio Muratori (*Fig. 17*). Ridolfi's work is characterized by a great solidity of structure and freedom in both plan and volume; the Quaroni project, through the elegance of its critical approach, seems to redeem the prevailing formal vulgarity and the vacuum that the architect must have felt due to the rationalist repression of a sense of history.

We can mention two important ideological movements which arose between 1936 and 1938: the first tended to recognize the structural aspect of the architectural problem in the area of urban planning. Bruno Zevi wrote in his *Storia dell'architettura moderna* (1950):

> The Italian tragedy does not exist so much in architecture as in town planning. There are some nice buildings in the University of Rome, but the over-all effect is one of monumentalism. For every ten modern buildings in Rome, we have the Plan of 1931, the frenetic demolitions, the ruination of the Borghi, and the

15. *Mario Ridolfi: Post office, Piazza Bologna, Rome, 1933, interior.*

16. *Mario Ridolfi: Apartment house, Via S. Valentino, Rome, 1936–37.*

17. *Saverio Muratori, Ludovico Quaroni: Competition for the Pretura Unificate, Rome, 1936, model.*

scandal of the Via della Conciliazione [a major street leading toward St. Peter's, for which parts of Rome's historic center were demolished].

In 1933, Luigi Piccinato and his group won the competition for the planning of the new city of Sabaudia with a very daring project (*Fig. 18*). In 1936, the Quaroni group proposed a project rigorously conceived in terms of the rationalist principles of housing, for the new city of Aprilia. In the same year, however, the Petrucci housing estate of Rome was built in rough, folklike architecture; it became the most reactionary expression of Mussolini's slogan, "going to the people." In 1938, the rationalists in Milan published in *Casabella* a plan for the Milano Verde district, a theoretical project for a neighborhood in a park, and from that day on the magazine as a whole was devoted to that area, which became the focus of Pagano's

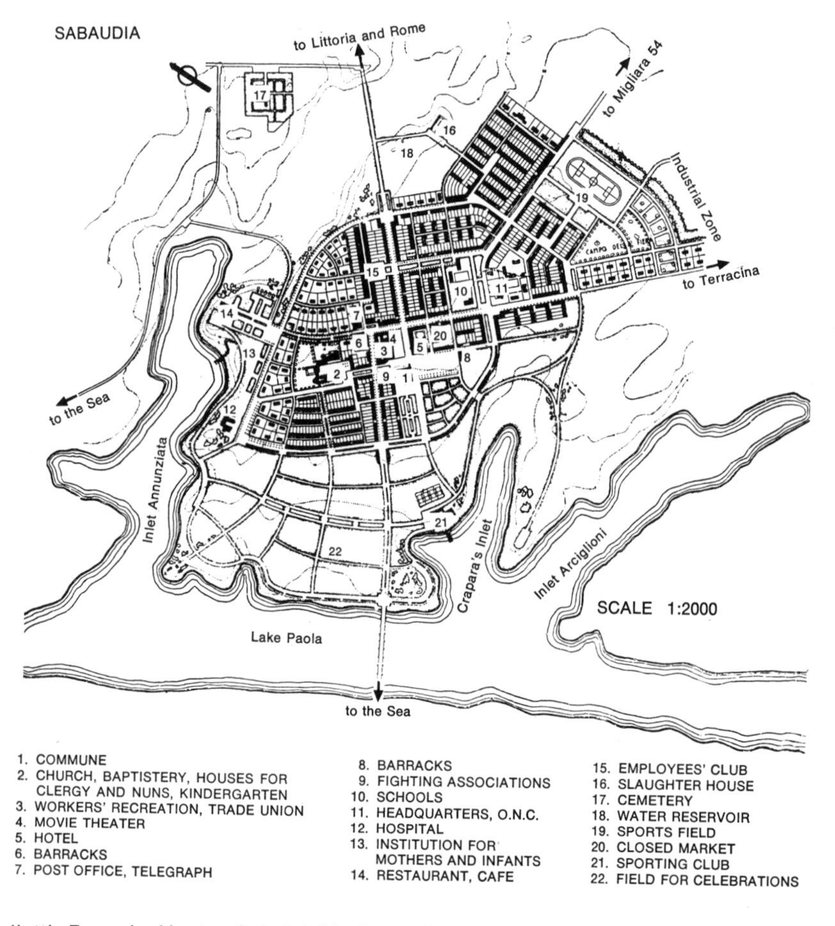

18. *Gino Cancellotti, Eugenio Montuori, Luigi Piccinato, Enrico Scalpelli: Sabaudia, 1933, plan.*

19. *Giuseppe Pagano: Faculty of Economics, Bocconi University, Milan, 1937–40.*

20. *Gianluigi Banfi, Ludovico Belgiojoso, Enrico Peressutti, Ernesto N. Rogers (B.B.P.R.): Aosta, Val d'Aosta, 1937, regional plan.*

polemics. In 1937, he had built the Faculty of Economics building at Bocconi University in Milan (*Fig. 19*). Also in 1937, Adriano Olivetti entrusted the young Gianluigi Banfi, Lodovico Belgiojoso, Enrico Peressutti, and Ernesto N. Rogers (B.B.P.R.), together with Piero Bottoni, Luigi Figini, and Gino Pollini, with the study for the first comprehensive Italian plan for the Val d'Aosta region in northwest Italy (*Fig. 20*). The result was highly interesting as a methodological experiment because it was a comprehensive study of socioeconomic and architectural elements.

The second movement rising between 1936 and 1938 occurred within Italian rationalism and tended to express the trend's theoretical and ideological problems. By now, having given up all ideas of winning the struggle for public approval, the rationalists turned to elaborating a rationalist critique which would include all the interrelations between the actual and the traditional environment, on a completely different level from the nationalistic arguments of the academicians. In 1938, in Alessandria in Piedmont, Ignazio Gardella, in his project for the Antituberculosis Dispensary (*Fig. 21*), for the first time employed techniques and materials drawn directly from the local tradition. His use of exposed brick and brick grillwork, and of a color other than white, is derived from the spontaneous architec-

21. *Ignazio Gardella: Antituberculosis Dispensary, Alessandria, 1936–38.*

22. *Gianluigi Banfi, Ludovico Belgiojoso, Enrico Peressutti, Ernesto N. Rogers (B.B.P.R.): Sun Therapy Colony, Legnano, 1939.*

23. *Carlo Mollino: Società Ippica Torinese, Turin, 1938, drawing.*

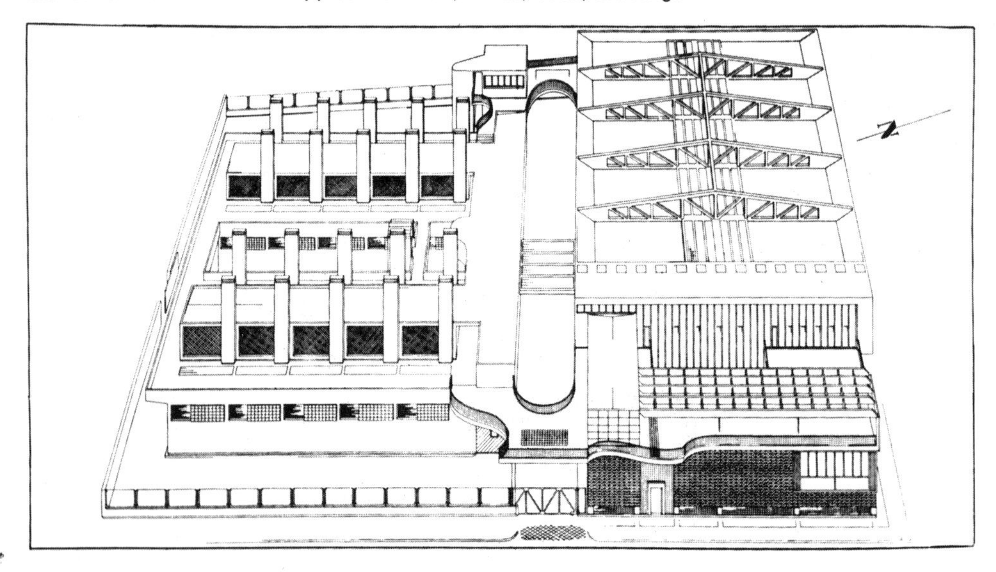

ture of the Paduan valley. The B.B.P.R., with the Sun Therapy Colony in Legnano (*Fig. 22*), and Carlo Mollino with the beautiful Società Ippica Torinese (*Fig. 23*) opened a critical dialogue with the International Style "white architecture" of the 1920's with remarkable results. These buildings proved that one could be modern with unusual forms that were not stylistically rationalist.

In the meantime, what became of the representatives of the Milanese 900? The members of this movement took four different directions, often simultaneously: at times they were preoccupied by the monumental rhetoric involved in the glorification of the "new Rome"; at times they were involved in formal simplification tending toward rationalism—as was Gio Ponti in the Montecatini office building (*Fig. 24*) in Milan—or they followed the Dutch models or the late German expressionists—as exemplified in the apartment building for the Piazza Repubblica in Milan (*Fig. 25*); at times they put forward neoclassicism as a nominal expression of the northern industrial middle class, despising fascism in favor of mass appeal; at times, finally, they sought, in partisan struggles, a happy, optimistic, Mediterranean "Italian style" of architecture, following Gio Ponti's slogan (*Fig. 26*).

24. *Antonio Fornaroli, Gio Ponti, Eugenio Soncini: Montecatini office building, Milan, 1939.*

25. *Giovanni Muzio: Apartment building, Piazza della Repubblica, Milan, 1936.*

26. *Emilio Lancia and Gio Ponti: House, ramparts of Porta Venezia, Milan, 1934.*

The last act in the defeat of rationalism in Italy may be said to have been the episode of E.U.R. 42. After a most unfortunate choice of site, for political reasons based on the idea of making Rome a great Mediterranean port, the plans were to have been drawn up by a group composed of Piacentini, Pagano, Piccinato, Luigi Vietti, and Ettore Rossi. But the result was disastrously monumental in its urban design and highly corrupt architecturally (*Fig. 27*). Some very clever architects gave in to the notorious columns, and only the B.B.P.R. built a truly modern building—the small post office.

Concealed behind his supposed technical neutrality, Pier Luigi Nervi, in the years following the construction of the Berta Stadium in Florence in 1932, built some of his best works (*Fig. 28*) and the first concrete stores.

However, what was the use, then, of buildings pleasing to modern taste? Conditions deteriorated rapidly: *Casabella* was forced to stop publication in 1943 by order of the government, and nearly all the rationalists joined the political underground. Terragni died prematurely at age 39; Raffaele Giolli, Gianluigi Banfi, and Guiseppe Pagano were arrested and then deported to German concentration camps, where they died in 1945. What had been a "problem of style" became a "problem of death and freedom." Many paid dearly for their errors and their doubts.

27. *Giuseppe Pagano, Marcello Piacentini, Luigi Piccinato, Ettore Rossi, Luigi Vietti: E.U.R. 42, Rome, 1942.*

28. *Pier Luigi Nervi: Reinforced concrete hangar, Orbetello, 1938.*

ARCHITECTURE OF THE POSTWAR RECONSTRUCTION 1944–1950

IN order to undertake an analysis of Italian architecture of the immediate postwar period, it is necessary to confine the discussion essentially to the two most important centers of Italian life—Rome and Milan. Rome, an essentially administrative city, with its poor outlying districts, is a filter, rather than a goal of interior migration and lacked, in 1945, any substantial rationalist architectural tradition. In addition, the Roman architects did not have private patrons, working as they did in the center of political power. Milan, on the other hand, is an industrial city with predominantly private customers; the harsh experience of the resistance was linked with a strong tradition of battles for modern architecture. This continuity with the rationalist tradition had begun to assert itself and joined the notion of resistance to fascism during the war.

In 1944, the C.I.A.M. (Congrès Internationaux d'Architecture Moderne, founded in 1928) created the first plan for the reconstruction of Milan, the A.R. Plan. It proposed for the first time the use of freeways and, at their crossing, the placement of a directional center to alleviate the functional burden of the historic center. In 1945, the Movement for Architectural Studies (M.S.A.) was established; it consisted of a group of architects claiming to belong to the modern movement and opposing the remaining academicians. In 1946, *Casabella* resumed publication for a brief period, dedicating its third issue to the work of Giuseppe Pagano. The seventh C.I.A.M. was held in Bergamo in 1949. Also in 1946, Ernesto N. Rogers took Gio Ponti's place as editor of *Domus*. "The problem," wrote Rogers in his editorial in the first issue of *Domus* (subtitled "The House of Man"), "is one of forging a taste, a technique, a morality, as different manifestations of the same problem: the problem of building a society."

This prolongation of the rationalist movement reached its most synthesized architectural expression with the B.P.R. monument (*Fig. 29*), dedicated to those who had died in concentration camps—dedicated therefore, above all, to Giuseppe Pagano, Gianluigi Banfi, Raffaello Giolli, Giorgio Beltrami, and Giorgio Labo, the rationalist architects who had died during the resistance. During the two years of Rogers' editorship, *Domus* acted primarily as a medium for universalizing Italian culture and for asserting the architect's intention of sharing in the general cultural activity. At the opposite pole, *Metron*, first published in 1945 in Rome and under the editorship of Bruno Zevi, Luigi Piccinato, and Silvio Radiconcini, concentrated,

29. *Ludovico Belgiojoso, Enrico Peressutti, Ernesto N. Rogers (B.P.R.): Monument to the victims of concentration camps, Milan, 1946.*

especially in its first two years, on problems of national reconstruction and particularly on urban planning.

The continuity of the rationalist movement in Milan and in northern Italy in general prevailed throughout the years 1948–1950. The rationalists still battled against an antimodern majority which, for instance, had complete control of the universities until 1946, when a group of students started the A.L.S.A. (Free Society of Architecture Students). They organized their own discussion groups and classes in opposition to official education. The rationalist architects still took a political stand very much in agreement with the Italian left wing.

The eighth Triennale opened in 1947 under the direction of Piero Bottoni. It was totally involved in coping with the problems of national reconstruction and in analyzing the needs of lower-income housing. Bottoni and others began the first experimental lower-class neighborhood in Milan—the Q.T.-8 (eighth Triennale quarter; *Fig. 30*)—but the attempt to transfer rationalist language, up to then associated with the cultural elite, to public housing was handicapped by the failure to see the need of reconsidering that language. The eighth Triennale resulted in a book by Irenio Diotallevi and Francesco Marescotti, *Il Problema Sociale, Economico e Construttivo dell'Abitazione* (1948). It was a book of research on different types of houses and also a sociopolitical declaration in the tradition of the students of the modern German movement; it was also—as a parallel to the National Research Institute's *Manuale dell'Architetto* (1946)—an attempt at codifying the constructional, craft experience, which was the only one which seemed likely to be realized in Italy at that time. The latter book, edited and sponsored by Mario Ridolfi in Rome, is the key to an understanding of at least ten years of Italian architecture and its expressive and technological structure.

The R.I.M.A. (Riunione Italiana Mostre Arredamento) exhibition held in Milan in 1946 showed that the architects of Milan were preoccupied with home furnishings, in the first attempt at applying the new principles of design to Italian furniture. In 1948, architects participated in many important city planning projects in Turin, Milan, Genoa, Reggio-Emilia (see page 54), and others. These attempts were often similar as to method, as the idea was to provide an overall basis for reconstruction. In the same year, the first studies for the regional planning project in Piedmont were undertaken. Also in 1948, C.I.A.M. in Milan presented a joint proposal for the Milan central business district. All these efforts were soon frustrated by changing political conditions and by the awareness of many differences within the modern movement, but they showed that the architects of the first generation of rationalism were committed to major issues.

In 1949, the magazine *Urbanistica* resumed publication under the editorship of Giovanni Astengo, and at the same time *Comunità* was founded, a magazine which was to greatly influence Italian urban studies, in the Mumfordian sense of community. The sponsor of both magazines, Adriano Olivetti, was the great patron of modern Italian architecture. All in all, what was lacking in the period, which can be considered the only period of realism in Italian architecture, was an adequate commitment to the renewal of the language of forms which could not be changed easily from a prewar avant-garde position to fit the new Italian reality. (By reality is meant the totality of elements available objectively to the artist. Realism tends to mirror, through art, this reality rather than to create a new reality.) But the presence of opposition made modern architects seem unified while they were in fact about to show their many points of discord.

What were the concrete accomplishments of architecture in this period? They were few in number, but nonetheless significant. The old academic administration, which had banded with the previous political regime, easily reformed itself in the official organization, as

30. *Piero Bottoni, Ezio Cerutti, Vittorio Gandolfi, Gino Pollini, Mario Pucci, Aldo Putelli, Morini: Q.T.-8 neighborhood, Milan, 1946–60, plan.*

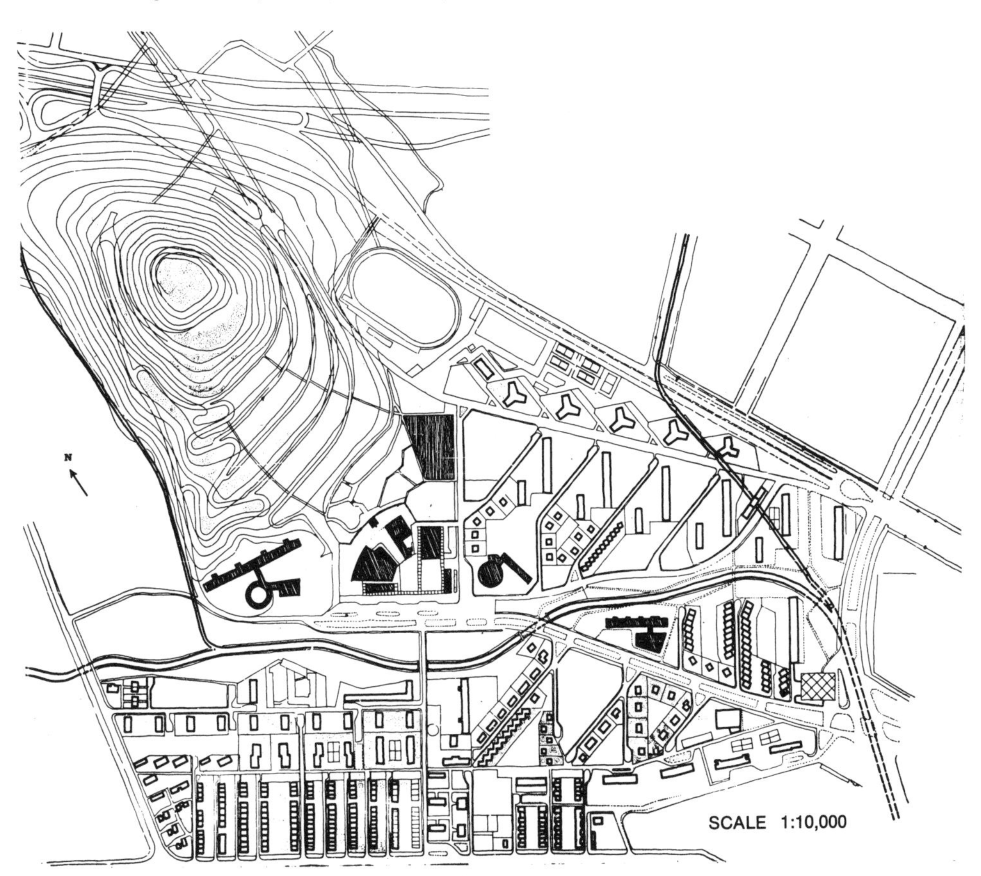

well as in the schools; while industry looked for faster and less ideologically awkward creative solutions, which were perhaps more technically advanced than the Italian architects could offer at the time. However, the second generation of modern architects, those who were just beginning their practice, established a closer contact with the client, particularly with the private client, even if they had to betray their ideological commitment when faced with their client's stylistic prejudices.

The most remarkable accomplishments of the 1950's were the works of B.P.R.—for their cultural aims, for their architectural qualities, and for the group's commitment to low-cost housing. Luigi Figini and Gino Pollini applied the research of the rationalist period to the quantitative problems of reconstruction; some minor work (interior decoration, stores, small homes) as well as the very gifted work of Carlo Mollino. Above all, there was the reconstruction of the Palazzo Bianco in Genoa by Franco Albini (*Fig. 31*) which, with its sensitive and abstract rigor, can be considered the archetype of the best Italian architecture up to 1950.

31. *Franco Albini: Gallery, Palazzo Bianco, Genoa, 1951, reconstruction.*

The situation in Rome, as mentioned, had entirely different roots, and was completely transformed by that extraordinary cultural organizer, Bruno Zevi. After return from political exile in the United States, Zevi published *Verso un'Architettura Organica* (1945), and over the years he made a fundamental contribution to the criticism and historiography of modern Italian architecture, bringing it once more into the international world of ideas. In 1950, he published his *Storia dell'architettura moderna*, the first such book to appear in Italy since Nikolaus Pevsner's *Pioneers of Modern Design, from William Morris to Walter Gropius*, which had been translated into Italian in 1946. As well as founding the magazine *Metron* in 1945, Zevi founded the Association for Organic Architecture (A.P.A.O.) in Rome. That association later opened branches in many other Italian cities.

Seen from the perspective of the present day, the polemics arising from the mistaken opposition of organic architecture to rationalism appear derived from the empirical psychology of the propaganda in favor of Frank Lloyd Wright. But the effect of the idea of interior space as matrix, in Benedetto Croce's sense, although not practical, was extremely valid, at least in theory. The A.P.A.O. suddenly embodied the tradition of the modern movement, where—as in Rome—there had been a trace of it before, and entered the battle against academicism which was stronger in Rome than in Milan. It should also be remembered that these were the years in which Pope Pius XII asked Marcello Piacentini to complete the plan of the Via della Conciliazione (1948–1950).

More important, A.P.A.O. opened the way for a body of creative impulses which had hitherto been repressed within rationalism's classical vocabulary. The important projects of the period had no direct connection with Wright. The two most important ones are the Monument of the Ardeatine Caves of 1944–1947 (*Fig. 32*) and the competition project for Rome's Termini railroad station (1947; *Fig. 33*) were the most representative as well as the most advanced products of the Roman school during this period. The old ties with certain aspects of late German expressionism (Hans Poelzig, Max Taut, Otto Bartning) were renewed, as in the model for the Prenestino Church by Quaroni (*Fig. 34*) and Ridolfi's I.N.A. Casa projects in Terni or on the Via Marco Polo in Rome, carrying on the tradition of the academic circles. The words "expressionism" and representationalism" were used again, although the declarations of the A.P.A.O. were united against the monumentalist concept. They read:

> Organic architecture is at once a socio-technical activity and an artistic activity directed towards creating the environment for a new democratic civilization: it is aimed at architecture for the human being, shaped to the human scale, and following the spiritual, psychological and contemporary needs of man as a part of society. Organic architecture is therefore the antithesis of the monumental architecture used to create official myths.

This declaration contains those elements of contradiction, with regard to already accomplished works, which brought about the dissolution of the A.P.A.O. The group had been weakened previously by the obstacles put in the way of its first large project, the establishment of I.N.A. Casa in 1949.

I.N.A. Casa (National Insurance Institute) was the organization through which the government promoted a massive financing plan for low-cost housing. The government entirely subsidized the buildings and assigned the projects to architects and engineers on the basis of competitions. I.N.A. Casa, which should have given builders, architects, and government the opportunity to build low-cost houses for workers, failed. Minority politics supported by the associations failed when faced with the problems of I.N.A. Casa which, under the

32. *Mario Fiorentino and others: Monument of the Ardeatine Caves, 1944–47.*

33. *Mario Fiorentino, Ludovico Quaroni, Mario Ridolfi, Cardelli: National competition for the Termini railroad station, Rome, 1947, drawing.*

34. *Ludovico Quaroni: Church, Prenestino quarter, Rome, 1949, model.*

sponsorship of the old bureaucratic class, ended up by weakening the debate on the distribution of work between corporation and clientele. At the same time, the cultural environment of Rome was propitious for the involvement of the architect in urban problems, while such involvement was gradually diminishing in the north.

In 1945, Luigi Piccinato was the only Italian architect who was adequately prepared to cope with urban problems, and his cultural contribution to *Metron*, followed by his association with the National Institute for Urban Studies, was of great importance. In 1946, Piccinato, together with Ridolfi, Franco Sterbini, Aldo Della Rocca, and Mario De Renzi, was put in charge of drawing up a plan for the traffic system in Rome. That plan grew into a true structural design for a new city and began a ten-year debate on Roman urban renewal. The architects split into two groups: those who were for speculation and those against speculation, those for planning and those against. On both fronts they were represented by stylistically modern architects.

The year 1948 was one of great resignations. Giovanni Michelucci in Florence left the Faculty of Architecture at the University, after having been involved in the controversy over the reconstruction of Florence. He had also written on this subject in the magazine *La Nouva Città*. A few years later in Naples, Luigi Cosenza, the best-known rationalist architect of that city, also left his university. We can therefore say that after 1948 the old academic leaders resumed control in the schools, except for the Venice Institute of Architecture, and that at the same time in the north the architects withdrew into profound and solitary meditation on the problem of expression, a withdrawal occasioned by their disappointment at the failure of their hopes for a progressive transformation of the sociopolitical structure. On the other hand, the Roman group turned from the problem in 1948, devoting all its energies toward planning; but such a commitment produced results only in neighborhood units, while the problems of public housing and urban scale were often neglected.

STRIVING FOR REALITY

THE years between 1951 and 1958 marked, for better or for worse, a turning point in the history of modern Italian architecture. This turning point can be called a "striving for reality"; its fundamental elements included striving for reality as understanding history and tradition, striving for reality as an aspect of left-wing, national, and popular ideology, and finally, striving for reality in the context of the existing environment or the geomorphology. These are, of course, three aspects of the same thing, since the philological study of the roots of the modern movement and the revision of the classical historiography of that movement are strictly tied to the revision of history (initiated by the modern movement) by integrating the local character of architecture, beginning with its folklike, popular aspects and the study of spontaneous, anonymous architecture ("architecture without architects," in Rudolfsky's phrase). These questions arose from the state of mind considering reality as a preexisting phenomenon and from the confusion involving such a consideration.

I should like to consider "striving for reality" in order to separate the architectural examples from the other phenomena of realism, or better, neorealism in Italian culture—literature, painting, theater, and, above all, films, which were Italy's most meaningful contribution at the international level. The fact that the realistic aspirations of Italian architecture could be realized—thanks in part to the economically sound nature of architectural discipline—only after 1950 (that is, after the political defeat of the Italian leftists in 1948, and the steady enlargement of the bureaucratic system of the Communist party) made the architects change their direction entirely. They ended up by devoting their energies not so much to the national reality as to a frequently sentimental image derived from outside factors: economic pressures, the proletariat, methods of production, political relationships, the function of the architect in society—these problems became themselves a reflection.

Realism in Italy ended in 1950; it ended in the magazine *Politecnico* and in the attempts of its editor, Elio Vittorini, to give it a direction to the left and a form adequate to avant-garde culture; it ended in the complicity in the Zdanovist policy in Soviet Russia; it ended with the coming to power of the Christian Democrats and the long-lasting splits in all party structures. The ghost of national progressive reality often evoked by the Italian architects after 1950 was still a symbol of the narrowness of an elitist culture incapable of accepting real isolation or becoming an authentic mass culture. Francesco Tentori, in his essay on "Fifteen Years of Italian Architecture" in *Casabella*, wrote:

> It was precisely for this reason that we spoke of individualistic fatalism. Because, in the best of instances, we believe that no architect has the illusion that he can stop, by exhibiting his rare works, the irresistible process of the crumbling and substitution of values. It is therefore purely and simply a matter of the division of the responsibilities pertinent to the present chaotic situation, for what that is worth.

This applied particularly to those architects who thought they could escape this architectural narrow-mindedness and hide behind empty formalism—an ambiguous reality made up of compromise and imagination, of theories rather than of substantialities, of economic needs rather than of action. This was true of our "exportable" formalists, of whom "other countries are so envious," who, "floating on a poetry of indifference," contributed toward combining the heritage of the modern vocabulary with the most reactionary aspects of land speculation, the destruction of historical centers, the despoiling of the landscape, or who transformed the ideological involvement of modern architecture into a practical commitment whose hallmark was efficient production. It must be acknowledged that this battle for realism in Italy was waged mainly by architects who, for the most part, belonged to the progressive political left, even though they thoughtlessly adhered to the propaganda of the Stalinist avant-garde, and through aesthetic imitation separated form from ideology. Perhaps they were afraid to lose contact with proletarian reality, which seemed to be embodied only in new methods of reaching the masses.

In addition, the issue of modern architecture and national tradition was brought up by the younger generation. This issue was openly set forth for the first time at a meeting of architecture students at Rome in 1954. The debate was reopened in June, 1955, at a meeting of the M.S.A. in Milan, since this group was by then in a position to offer a large number of modern examples and statements. The same obstinate emphasis on structural details was characteristic of architecture during those years. Such emphasis, on the one hand, was tied in with the architectural-artisan tradition in Italy and, on the other hand, was applicable to a language which was easily comprehended by the masses, as well as being more perceptible and more able to articulate architectural form.

This turned the practical precepts of the *Manuale dell'Architetto* into an expressive vocabulary. Technology as an outgrowth of the system had to be exorcized; every possibility of considering it as an end in itself had to be set aside; thus, during those years it was impossible to understand its real meaning in relation to human endeavor. Moreover, popular and national culture had to find its own autonomous, expressive language, in opposition to that of the bourgeois elite, without really believing that such language could form part of the avant-garde movement.

Manfredo Tafuri, the most brilliant critic of Italian architecture in this period, wrote:

> The proud declaration of autonomy contrasts with the recognition of a language made up of traditional elements not pertinent to a bourgeois culture, yet sounding like a glorification of history, a history which is not the history of a lower class nor of an upwardly mobile class, but rather the history of an oppressed, inferior class: more categorically, a folklore, outside any healthy consideration of realism.

The most representative culminating episode in this striving to reality is, I believe, the popular neighborhood unit of I.N.A. Casa Tiburtino 3° in Rome (*Fig. 35*). This was the work not only of Ludovico Quaroni and Mario Ridolfi, the most remarkable architects of postwar Rome, but also of the younger generation who graduated

35. *Ludovico Quaroni, Mario Ridolfi, Carlo Aymonino, and others: I.N.A. Casa Tiburtino quarter, Rome, 1950–54.*

after the war. If this neighborhood today seems almost grotesque ("the city-town of the baroque," as Quaroni called it in his own self-criticism), it nevertheless represents in an exemplary way the hopes and contradictions of Italian culture during those years. Its provincialism; the attempt to embody aspirations toward socialism in a progressive way; the conformity to the left; the contradiction between concept and building; the confused but strong impulse away from the ideal and abstract toward a renewal of formal communication in architecture, the desire to communicate through architecture the feelings and errors common to a whole generation. All these were features which also contributed to the success of the housing estate—which were of a different order from the Tiburtino quarter—on the Viale Etiopia built by Ridolfi in Rome between 1950 and 1952 (*Fig. 36*). This is the climax that Italian architecture reached in its striving toward reality. It approached directly the difficulties inherent in urban structures without ignoring the conditions of population density and stratification, which offer advantages as well as inconveniences. This accomplishment presented a formal solution which was popular, despite its technological and typological aspects, which were strictly circumscribed by the linguistic structure; thus, the work was transformed into a popular epic while still remaining faithful to the modern movement.

From 1950 to 1958 Ridolfi was active in a conscious and fully practical way. From the apartments of Cerignola (*Fig. 37*) to the prison

36. *Mario Ridolfi (with Wolfgang Frankl): Apartment buildings, Viale Etiopia, Rome, 1950–52.*

37. *Mario Ridolfi (with Wolfgang Frankl): I.N.A. Casa quarter, Cerignola, 1950.*

38. *Ludovico Quaroni, Luigi Agati, Federico Gorio, Piero Maria Lugli, Michele Valori: La Martella, Matera, 1949.*

of Nuoro, to the Ivrea house, he expanded his experiments by genuinely running the risk of expressing himself and making mistakes.

The opposite pole of such attempts to relate to a popular architectural language lay in Quaroni's experiment of the Martella neighborhood near Matera (1951; *Fig. 38*), which was built within the context of the disputed agricultural reform in southern Italy of those years. (The new town of La Martella, in southern Italy, is an agricultural center in a large landed estate subdivided into small lots. It reveals the importance of the southern problem, which still divides Italy. The North is a symbol of industrial prosperity, and the South a symbol of agricultural underdevelopment.) At the root of this neighborhood experiment, which was built according to a community plan and based on a formal reevaluation of spontaneous architecture, lay the issue of sociological research. This sociological, community approach was greatly to influence the building of subsidized neighborhoods (from Cutro to Borgo Venusio, from San Basilio (*Fig. 39*) to the Falchera, built in Turin by Giovanni Astengo's group). It seemed to have been based substantially on more objective criteria than those of the Tiburtino quarter, but that was an illusion.

It soon became clear that such an approach was intended to preserve the social structure and underdevelopment. The popular forms were no longer merely those of the conceptual architectural

39. *Mario Fiorentino: San Basilio quarter, Rome, 1956.*

language of the Tiburtino, but its important elements are the interior court and the neighborhood unit. The topological elements of the "village" were analyzed and reformulated in density patterns and services, a process borrowed from Swedish and Danish architecture, very influential in Italy during those years. The influence of northern neoempiricism, critically reevaluated by Zevi and accepted as the prime example of a modest but civilized and emotional solution, was very great throughout this period. For example, in 1951 Ignazio Gardella designed an apartment house for the Borsalino employees in Alessandria (*Fig. 40*), housing which was still influenced by Scan-

40. *Ignazio Gardella: Apartment house for Borsalino employees, Alessandria, 1953, detail.*

dinavian neoempiricism and to a large extent bound up with the neoclassical architecture.

The relation between bourgeois neoclassicism, as seen in the work of Gardella, and the needs of realistic architecture in construction and mass housing, gave rise to a particular version of the striving for reality, developed for the most part by L. Caccia Dominioni in Milan (*Fig. 41*), where the neoclassical tradition had already been supported by the architects of the Milanese 900. The factions in the Society of Engineers and Architects in Reggio-Emilia formed one of the most representative elements, on a formal and on a technical level. Backed by a tradition of structural sincerity and following the example of Manfredini and above all Franco Albini, with his apartment and office building in Parma (*Fig. 42*), as well as a well-characterized body of spontaneous local architecture, this group was instrumental in promoting the architecture of the entire region.

Interest in spontaneous architecture had long existed in Italy. Since Giuseppe Pagano's and Guarniero Daniel's book, *Architettura Rurale Italiana* (1936), this architecture had been considered as

41. *L. Caccia Dominioni: Orphanage and convent, Milan, 1955.*

42. *Franco Albini: I.N.A. office building, Parma, 1953.*

naturally connected with rationalist architecture, inasmuch as it related the natural and functional styles of building. The ninth Triennale (1951) devoted substantial research to spontaneous architecture and dedicated a remarkable exhibition to it. Its extraordinary formal repertory had for many years a direct influence on the attempts of Italian architecture to make contact with the working class.

The other approach of the striving for reality—the philological and historical one—arose during those years in *Casabella.* This magazine had resumed publication in 1954, under the editorship of Ernesto N. Rogers. A new generation of architects grew up with *Casabella*, a generation characterized by their proposal of criticism and history as dialogue, by their use of theory as dialogue, by their consideration of architecture as an area of knowledge, and through their refusal to separate theory from practice. A few years later, a new group, inspired by the same interest in criticism, was formed, led by Paolo Portoghesi in Rome. This group was highly influenced by the brilliant, if reactionary, ideas of Saverio Muratori.

On the ideological level, three important and contradictory sources gave rise to critical debates among the new generation writing in *Casabella.* First of all, a book by Giulio Carlo Argan, *Walter Gropius e la Bauhaus* (1951), analyzed the elements of Bauhaus culture from the Marxist point of view. This was a study which gave an historical context to the avant-garde, which had been hidden and crushed by an absolute contemporaneity. Another important influence was the result of Theodor W. Adomo's criticism of the consumer society, *Minima Moralia* (which was translated at that time in Italy), and also to the reinterpretation of Marx by the phenomenological school, led by Enzo Paci. Finally, due to the increasing strength of the middle class, rationalism appeared as empty of its revolutionary potential and as an ally of the class in power. In 1963, Paolo Portoghesi wrote in his catalogue of the Aquila exhibition (*Aspetti dell'Arte Contemporanea*), at which the results of those years were shown: "Neo-liberty was born" between the "poles of Turin and Milan, with Novara acting as a go-between" (*Fig. 43*). The people of Turin, mainly Catholic, had to return to the surviving bourgeois values and to acknowledge the responsibility of that class faced with structural transformation. This meant proposing the adjustment of the new social structure to the control of a more progressive, European bourgeoisie. For the Milanese, who were for the most part Marxists, neo-Liberty was a protest, a return to a situation already considered negative, a kind of ironic view of the Italian bourgeoisie as still restrained by pre-capitalistic prejudices and trying to condense fifty years of the European cultural experience.

It can be clearly seen that these themes did not share an approach we have previously described: that is, the denial of folklike elements and the natural, dialectical, spontaneous tradition, in favor of a cultivated link with the progressive elements in a still unrealized

43. *Vittorio Gregotti, Ludovico Meneghetti, Giotto Stoppino: T. L. store, Novara, 1955.*

44. *Giorgio Raineri, addition to an elementary school, Turin, 1957–58.*

national Italian culture, which had never arisen after the decline of local traditions (*Fig. 44*). The European aspect of the bourgeois Art Nouveau and the neomediaevalism of Camillo Boito, the Lombard neoclassical tradition in architecture, or architecture as political commitment—these are the elements on which this group for the most part based its attempt to establish a relationship which today we can perhaps call determinist and deductive, somewhere between ideology and architectural language. The possibilities of using these principles directly in architecture were very limited, and the number of executed buildings small, but their influence was extremely widespread. However, since this group's protest did not propose a real pedagogical method, its influence was, in the end, damaging, particularly in view of the frivolously pleasing nature of some examples.

Instead, the environmental theory was the cultural medium in which the architects of the first generation of rationalism worked in the realm of a search for reality. The generation in between, with the exception of Vico Magistretti, was less sensitive to the historical problem, sheltered as it was by its adherence to matters of production, in which the architect's artistic involvement implied an involvement of his professional morality. The M.S.A. was the arena for the debate between supporters of the two positions, but Rogers' unquestionable authority stood between their strivings for reality. In his series of editorials in *Casabella* between 1954 and 1955 ("Responsibility to Tradition," "Pre-existence of the Environment and Practical Themes," "The Tradition of Italian Modern Architecture"), and later with the publication of Number 215 of *Casabella* and his book *Esperienza dell'Architettura* (1958), Rogers set forth the theory of the problem of the environment as a connecting element between modern architecture and history and tradition. On the one hand, this attitude contrasted with that of the rationalist architects, and on the other hand, it gave rise to intense polemics within the new generation writing in *Casabella.*

The thesis of environmental preexistence seemed to call for divorcing the object as object; to situate it in an environment, as a first encounter with reality, but it also seemed to call for and produce an alteration of terms by introducing new elements into the classical methodology of rationalism; these elements were history and tradition, which enriched the sources of the "structuring" of the object. (This need to return to history was later very deeply felt on an international level, by Louis Kahn, with his continuing explicit references to Roman architecture and French neoclassicists, as well as by suggestions of prehistoric elements in the later work of Le Corbusier, such as Ronchamp or Chandigarh.)

When Walter Gropius moved to the United States, returning to history was seen as a problem of dependence on local traditions. We have already seen, moreover, that this attitude had its roots in Italian architecture, in the work of Luigi Figini, Gino Pollini and

45. *Giovanni Michelucci: Church, Collina, 1954.*

46. *Giovanni Michelucci: Borsa Merci, Pistoia, 1950.*

Ignazio Gardella, and the B.B.P.R. before the war, and in the postwar works of Franco Albini, such as the Rifugio Pirovano, a hotel at Cervinia. We cannot completely accept, however, the belief that a substantial discrepancy existed between this attitude and the architect's attempt to protect historical centers and valuable sites.

In this perspective, it can be asserted that the best Italian architects of the first generation of rationalism flourished during the early fifties: Giovanni Michelucci, with his Collina church (*Fig. 45*) and the earlier Borsa Merci (Commodity Exchange) in Pistoia (1950; *Fig. 46*); Gardella, with his Hotel Punta San Martino (in collaboration with Marco Zanuso) (*Fig. 47*), the Zattere house in Venice (*Fig. 48*), and some furnishings; Franco Albini, with his Museum of the Tesoro di San Lorenzo (*Fig. 49*), which is certainly one of the most beautiful works of postwar Italian architecture, and his project for the department store La Rinascente in Rome (*Fig. 50*) (particularly his first and more interesting version, which was so deeply influenced by the metal structures of the nineteenth century); Giuseppe Samonà, with the I.N.A.I.L. (National Institute for Industrial Accidents) building in Venice; and finally, the B.P.R. who, with the Torre Velasca skyscraper (*Fig. 51*), symbolized the research into memory and tradition and simultaneously created an object which received enormous international opposition. As we have seen, precisely because this realism was nothing more than the projection of the idea of reality,

47. *Ignazio Gardella, Marco Zanuso, Guido Venezioani: Hotel Punta San Martino (Arenzano), Genoa, 1958.*

48. *Ignazio Gardella: House at the Zattere, Venice, 1957.*

49. *Franco Albini: Museum of the Tesoro di San Lorenzo, Genoa, 1956, interior.*

what was produced was an image, a protest and a demonstration of error, rather than an optimistic proposal; it was an extreme attempt to consider architecture as a protest. The results of this realism very often destroyed any intention of methodological adherence to the modern movement and overwhelmed the designers with doubts and fears.

At a M.S.A. debate in 1955, Albini asserted:

> Man's history is not nature's history, where anything can happen: it is made by man, who by his continuous, conscious action keeps altering its course. The continuity of events is not a tradition in itself; it becomes so within the conscience of man. . . . Tradition as a collective conscience, as an acknowledgment; regard for tradition means the recognition of collective control of public opinion, of a control from the people. Tradition, as discipline, is an opening to freedom of the imagination, to temporary methods, to mediocre errors. . . .

Notwithstanding these assertions, however, the architect had by now discovered the nature of his compromise: he must act without being. He had discovered that the lens of his own subjectivity crudely reflected such compromise, and that the more acute and penetrating the image, the greater the reflected impracticability of an entire culture.

50. *Franco Albini and Franca Helg: La Rinascente, Rome, 1961.*

51. *Ludovico Belgiojoso, Enrico Peressutti, Ernesto N. Rogers (B.P.R.): Torre Velasca, Milan, 1958.*

PROFESSIONAL, POLITICAL, AND PRODUCTIVE CONTEXTS

AS the previous chapter has shown, one of the most important efforts in the striving for reality is represented by low-income housing. The fundamental aspects of this realistic outlook have been mentioned in connection with the Tiburtino and Martella neighborhoods (see page 52). These examples, including the activities of I.N.A. Casa, influenced Italy for ten years, and they were also responsible for the foundation of G.E.S.C.A.L. (Management of Homes for Workers), the organization which took over the responsibility for low-income housing in 1963. The substantial disorganization and weakness of the institutional patronage, by the inability to coordinate on a technological level and to organize on a local level; emphasis laid on housing construction instead of on public services and infrastructures, all this influenced even private reconstruction and land speculation. Indeed, a characteristic of Italian reconstruction was the priority of land speculation over building speculation, since local organizations did not control the land market, neither through modern legislative means nor through political arrangements. This was a restraint on the building industry, since any technical industrial building improvement appeared irrelevant compared to the profit from land. Reconstruction thus lost any democratic control, as did the architects themselves, who had counted on such control.

The traditional Italian mistrust of modern culture isolated the architect and made his services a luxury item, which put the responsibility for reconstruction in the hands of the civil engineer and the draftsman. No one sought out the architect for what he was able to offer; no one paid him for his work: his role was somewhere between that of a servant and an antagonist, and his professional standing was a humiliation. The lack of a sense of responsibility toward the state and the carelessness of local organization made private enterprise the only organized body to take command. The result was the disorderly development of the underprivileged areas, the expedient rush to combine formally unassimilated themes and to pile them on inadequate sites, lacking public services and infrastructures—which were turned over to the local public organizations, and the creation—without foreseeing the possibility of an organic locality—of squatter's areas (*bidonvilles*) at a high cost all around the city. The bourgeoisie created the condominium and the "palazzina" (a building in which each owner has more than one floor, giving the effect of superimposed villas), and with these standardized buildings, which lacked beauty of structure and landscaping, invaded the countryside and put up slums for the well-to-do which differed from those of the poor only in their more luxurious facades and the presence of many automobiles. No less serious is the situation in the suburbs of industrial cities like Milan, where the lack of planning creates vast problems.

Urban centers were equally damaged before planning laws could be enacted. Speculation was rampant. There were no pretenses, not even formal ones, to anything else. All this resulted in the scandal of the buildings at Por Santa Maria in Florence, the shameful architecture of the Corso Vittorio Emanuele in Milan, the nonsensical concentration of buildings in Naples, the Parioli in Rome, which absurdly seemed to indicate the E.U.R. site as the only urban approach to Rome. The history of Rome's town plan from this point of view may serve as an example: in 1959, after four years of debate and struggle over the plan, modern culture was defeated. Michele Valori, one of the protagonists in the battle, wrote an article in *Urbanistica* (Numbers 28/29), entitled "Fare del proprio peggio" ("Doing One's Worst"), in which he said: "Our principal mistake was to begin by expecting to lose, and therefore to do nothing but avoid losing; an excessive lack of confidence in the power of public opinion." The opportunity given by Rome city planning was that for seeing who belonged on which side. One is forced to admit that the real supporters of the empty rationalism, which contained nothing but style and elegance, were the most closely allied with the speculators, and that this greatly contributed to confusing the architect's function, already affected by problems of expression.

If the city, with its brutal vitality, accumulates disorder and debris, rural areas, which are the basic nucleus of overpopulated Italy, languish and slowly deteriorate in the shadow of some useless and disastrous skyscraper (the false symbol of modern life), in the light of neon signs which have taken the place of the old street lamps. There are few schools, some houses, no hospitals; very few productive structures fit the locale. As soon as economic conditions improve, the struggle shifts from urban centers to the landscape, which tourism has now made into a lucrative asset. This kind of speculation is fumbling in the dark and destroying its precious capital. Four thousand kilometers (about 1,820 miles) of coastline are destroyed without a trace of coordinated planning, uselessly spoiled merely because of planning oversights. The few important attempts of any quality, such as the Gardella plan for Arenzano in northern Italy (see *Fig. 47*), and that of Marcello D'Olivo for Manocore in the Gargano province of southern Italy are rapidly overwhelmed by speculation. And this is not all. The incessant destruction of wooded areas, the failure of natural waterway conservation projects, the lack of concern for erosion, all this will lead to disasters like the Florence floods, the periodic flooding of the Po Valley, and the gradual sinking of Venice.

Antonio Cederna called his book *I Vandali in Casa* (1956). He was one of the most stubborn partisans of Italian landscape preservation, and in 1957 he created Italia Nostra, a society which, in spite of the ambiguity of many of its causes, contributed largely to bringing the problem of conservation before the public. The other coordinated element working against speculation is the National Institute of Urbanism, through its magazine *Urbanistica*, its annual meetings (Intercommunal Planning, 1956; The Preservation and Exploitation of Landscape, in Lucca in 1957; The Aspect of the City, Lecce, 1959; Proposal for an Urban Law, Rome, 1960; Programs for Economical Development and Urban Planning, Milan, 1962) and finally through its attempts to apply in Italy urban planning more modern than that envisaged in 1942.

What was the attitude of architects when faced with such a chaotic situation? As we have previously seen, some fell back on a formal protest, others argued as to whether town planning had priority over architecture; others, like Ludovico Quaroni, were divided between protest and political or legislative intervention; others believed in solving the problems by competing on the level of productive efficiency, which was being pressed on them by industry. They became suspicious of ideological compromise and attempted to set forth the necessity of neutrality where their profession was concerned, and of technicalism as an escape from those problems.

Meanwhile, almost everyone, although with widely different intentions, made way for the attempts at rationalization of construction, which emptied that approach of any social significance or understanding. Because of this need, some architects saw a way toward the renewal of the formal vocabulary of rationalism; some neighborhoods of I.N.A. Casa, from Harar in Milan (*Fig. 52*) to Bernabò Brea in Genoa (*Fig. 53*) to the Cesate district by Albini-Gardella B.P.R. showed a rationalistic continuity which symbolized rather than embodied the technological problem. On a linguistic level, realism generally tended to break with the unity of rationalistic formalism by emphasizing single parts, structural components, connective devices, by means of an analytic language in which the structural detail rather than the volume (determined by economic considerations) became the expressive matrix. A central aspect of that expressive research—one also found in present international architecture—was a critical discussion of the tradition of the modern movement which has obvious parallels in the mannerist discussions of the second half of the sixteenth century. A formal language so developed is exploited even in minor building. Such is the case with buildings four or five stories high, constructed with reinforced concrete frames and brick infilling, with floor-to-ceiling windows, doors, and frames, especially suited to the current semiartisanal building

52. *Luigi Figini, Gino Pollini, Gio Ponti: I.N.A. Casa quarter, Via Harar, Milan, 1951.*

53. *Luigi Carlo Daneri, L. Grossi Bianchi, Guilio Zappa: I.N.A. Casa residential unit, Villa Bernabò Brea, Genoa, 1953, plan.*

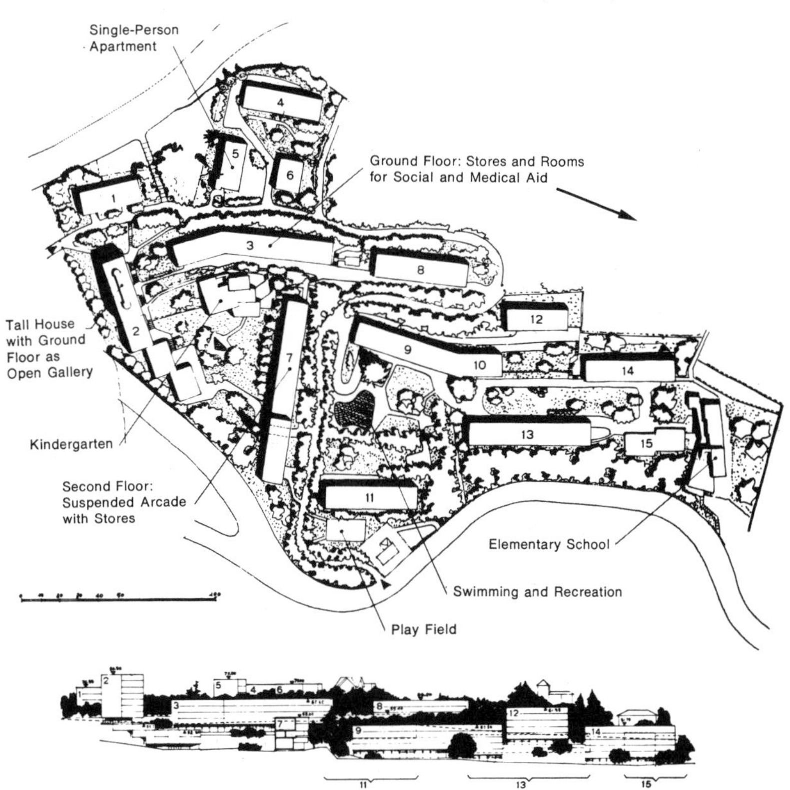

54. *Giuseppe Samonà: M.P.S. offices, Messina, 1958.*

55. *Vittorio Gregotti, Ludovico Meneghetti, Giotto Stoppino (Associated Architects of Novara): Apartment houses with prefabricated elements, Novara, 1959.*

56. *Angelo Mangiarotti: Houses with prefabricated elements, Marcianise, Caserta, 1962.*

57. *Michele Valori, Ezio Sgrelli, R. Donatelli: Apartment house, Milan, 1952.*

techniques, became an overtly manneristic compositional style which, however, sometimes reached real expressive nobility, as in the case of Ezio Sgrelli, Gian Emilio, Piero and Anna Monti, Gianpaolo Valenti, for instance.

The residential quarter of Via Cavedone in Bologna, for example, although still characterized by the old idea of the neighborhood unit in its very precise organization of detail and execution, reached a standard of finish superior to that of I.N.A. Casa and to anything produced by private speculators for more limited markets. This process was especially noteworthy on the expressive, as well as on the technical, level where semiprefabricated structures were concerned. On one hand, we have the experiments of Guiseppe Samonà (*Fig. 54*) and the Associated Architects of Novara (*Fig. 55*), who critically analyzed Auguste Peretti's experiments in prefabrication and the experiments of Angelo Mangiarotti who, through prefabrication, proposed a new expressive purism (*Fig. 56*); on the other hand, Mario Fiorentino and Michele Valori (*Fig. 57*) reapplied Mario Ridolfi's experiments in the Viale Etiopia.

It must be admitted that despite the lack of organization in the building industry, Italy over the past twenty years has produced some remarkable works, particularly with regard to reinforced concrete structures in which compressed and tensile functions are differentiated, which are still very rare and expensive in Italy. Riccardo Morandi achieved an international reputation through his use of

58. *Riccardo Morandi: Viaduct above Polcevera, Genoa.*

59. *Silvano Zorzi: Bridge on the Arno, Autostrada del Sòle, Incisa, Florence, 1963.*

60. *Giuseppe Raineri: Silos on the Stura, Turin, 1956.*

tie rods and central standing structures (*Fig. 58*). Following him, Silvano Zorzi (*Fig. 59*), Sergio Musumeci, Aldo Favini, Giuseppe Raineri (*Fig. 60*) and many others wished to give autonomous architectural qualities to buildings whose primary character was structural adventure.

The architect best known internationally for his work in reinforced concrete is Pier Luigi Nervi (*Fig. 61*). The rigorous continuity of his buildings seems to evade history. It is almost impossible and perhaps useless to give exact dates for Nervi's work, or to write a history of them. Nervi believes that structural forms are tending to a deductive fatality, beginning from objective conditions; he has what might be called a spiritual conception of architecture. This abstract rigor, this structural integrity, have at times made him appear insensitive to the significance of the total work. Sometimes he has chosen questionable collaborators (like Marcello Piacentini, the official Fascist architect and the strongest opponent of the modern movement); sometimes he was faced with dubious opportunities which did not allow him to produce a total work, but only fragments which inconspicuously revealed some strangely disastrous architectural facets. On this level, and perhaps also insofar as structural imagination was concerned, he reached his peak with the hangar at Orbetello, built in 1936 (see *Fig. 28*).

Often, a typological or technical opportunity offers the basis for the solution of problems: examples are the Thermoelectric Center designed by Samonà and the very high and remarkable level reached by Ezio Sgrelli when facing an industrial theme (*Fig. 62*).

61. *Pier Luigi Nervi: G.A.T.T.I. wool factory, Rome, 1953.*

62. *Ezio Sgrelli: Administration buildings of the Montesud, Brindisi, 1964.*

63. *Luigi Cosenza: Olivetti plant, Pozzuoli, Naples, 1955.*

64. *Luigi Figini and Gino Pollini: Olivetti plant, Ivrea, 1957.*

65. *Marco Zanuso: Olivetti plant, Buenos Aires, 1960.*

66. *Marcello Nizzoli and Mario Oliveri: E.N.I. office building, S. Donato Milanese, Milan, 1958.*

67. *Gio Ponti, Antonio Fornaroli, Alberto Rosselli, Giuseppe Valtolina, Egidio Dell'Orto, Pier Luigi Nervi, Arturo Danusso: Pirelli office building, Milan, 1961.*

Between 1951 and 1960, Adriano Olivetti engaged a series of well-known architects to build a group of factories—Luigi Cosenza in Naples (*Fig. 63*), Luigi Figini and Gino Pollini in Ivrea (*Fig. 64*), Marco Zanuso in Buenos Aires (*Fig. 65*) and Sao Paolo, Eduardo Vittoria in Ivrea. They were to work without restricting themselves to a homogeneous image. The accomplishment of Cosenza was almost domestic in scale; the example of Figini and Pollini was rigorously stereometric; Zanuso's attempt was proudly technological. Still, they formed a collective experiment articulating in a valuable way the few choices at their disposal. A modern factory is still something new for Italy, an area for demonstration rather than the development of a working environment. The architect's work is often included in the budget for public relations rather than in that for technical production. The problem is quickly solved before being tested; these procedures thus result in bad imitations of previous solutions, which have sprung up like mushrooms. Sometimes an attempt was made to redeem the work through style, usually an expressive modernism not too far from the "aerodynamism" of the 1930's. This line was fol-

68. *Vittoriano Viganò: Marchiondi Spagliardi Institute (for youth re-education), Milan, 1957.*

lowed by some clever architects, such as Marcello Nizzoli (*Fig. 66*), Gio Ponti (*Fig. 67*), Gian Luigi Giordani, and sometimes even Angelo Mangiarotti, who created forms on an international rather than a provincial level. In this sense, they achieved results of a certain elegance and beauty of form without scale, a sort of perfect calligraphy.

Special cases are those of Luciano Baldessari, whose Breda pavilion at the Milan Fair displayed a remarkable plastic invention; Paolo Soleri's ceramics factory near Naples; Vittoriano Viganò, whose violent language arose out of French sculptural experiments, lead him to a brutalist manner *ante letteram*, as in the Marchiondi Spagliardi Institute in Milan (*Fig. 68*); and the work of Enrico Castiglioni, an architect with an undoubtedly nervous talent for plastic-structural experiments (*Fig. 69*), who was also influenced by *L'architecture d'aujourd'hui.* Up to 1959, these experiments ran parallel to the ideological commitment of the striving for reality, and only after 1959 did a debate between the two sides once again break out.

69. *Enrico Castiglioni: Competition for the Sanctuary in Siracusa, 1957, model.*

THE CONTEMPORARY SCENE

THE year 1959 was one of crisis in those attitudes which we have called a "striving for reality": they are transformed in three different points of view. First, the relationship between ideology and language shifts in terms analogous to literary criticism and debate; the dependence of language on ideology, the aesthetic theory of Lakuo's which has led to a new interest in linguistic studies, and theories of information and mass communication are all strongly directed toward the problems of the experimental avant-garde. Second, architects and critics faced the problem of the new urban dimension; the concept of the neighborhood, which was in its turn derived from the tradition of the modern movement, is therefore put in doubt. Third, the impetus toward technological renewal rising from accomplishments in design and from the interest of big corporations in new methods of design and building (integral projects, prefabrication, rationalization of the construction site, and others). This growing interest in the rationalization of design, credit for which should go to the magazine *Superfici*, is linked to the great urban and regional opportunities, which led to the organization of interdisciplinary study centers and groups aiming to restate analytical methods and alternative hypotheses for territorial problems.

One of the elements which emphasized the crisis of methodology of urban problems and media was undoubtedly the mass immigration from south to north, from the Veneto to the industrial triangle, from valleys to plateaus, which took place during the years of the "Italian economic miracle," from 1957–1958 to 1961–1962. Not only were town structures a handicap during this phenomenon, but architectural culture did not realize that standardization and improvement of taste and consumption could no longer be approached in terms of "popular" culture, but rather in terms of "mass" culture.

The actual attempt at solutions to these problems was facilitated on the one hand by the establishment of interdisciplinary research centers, composed mainly of economic, sociological, and managerial disciplines, and supported by local organizations such as I.R.E.S. (Institute for Economic and Statistic Research of Piedmont, founded in 1959) and I.L.S.E.S. (Lombardy Institute for Economic and Statistical Studies, 1960). Giancarlo De Carlo organized a meeting of I.L.S.E.S. in 1962 on the "new dimension of the city," which was fundamental for establishing new concepts of "city-region" and "city-territory." These research centers were supposed to bring those who were only beginning to undertake regional town planning on a methodological level up to date, principally along American lines.

On the other hand, at the same time the question of a school of city planning arose and in Arezzo, Ludovico Quaroni began an experimental course. This course soon became a debate between two groups. One group aimed to combine political choices with urban choices, while the other aimed to apply scientific methods to "planning" in order to then present alternatives to the politicians. Among the intercommunal plans, the most complex and articulate experiment (although beset by political difficulties) was the P.I.M. (Intercommunal Plan for Milan), proposed by De Carlo and still in a process of evolution.

The attempt to bridge previous experiments and new problems was skillfully summarized in a phrase of Ernesto N. Rogers in *Casabella* in 1962: "the utopia of reality." This was an important and subtle idea which combined the two dialectical elements of Italian architectural culture: the striving through direct contact with the concrete experience of national reality, and the impetus toward a radical movement, toward experimental research. Rogers also recognized the need for new, antiprofessional university teachers who would shun the system and would concentrate on the future of research and on new classroom architectural experiments. A renewed interest in international experiments, mainly in England and the United States, where architectural culture reached its highest development, strongly contributed to this crisis and this change. These changes were further stimulated by perennial exchanges in various reviews and some international meetings.

What turned out to be the last meeting of C.I.A.M. and the first of Team 10 took place at Otterlo, Holland, in 1959. On this occasion, the Italian group—Gardella, Rogers, Vico Magistretti, and De Carlo—was confronted with the result of its own research in a difficult international debate. Italian architecture was harshly attacked; the attacks were legitimate but arose out of that critical indifference which so often equates modernism with flat roofs. Even De Carlo, who has opposed every form of historicism, was attacked for the evidence of historicism in his works, such as his building in the Spine Bianche quarter, in southern Italy.

After some years of polemics and efforts to create a national modern architecture, as well as to find a national way toward socialism, it is still clear that others are much further ahead of Italy; above all, the architectural culture of other nations, less exposed to political and ideological pressures, has not only become highly developed, but has also carried on a fluid methodological dialogue regarding its formative processes, a dialogue less committed but substantially more stubtle and perceptive than the Italian. It has been eventually more productive, in intent as well as *in toto.*

In 1959, Giuseppe Samonà published a book entitled *L'Urbanistica e l'Avvenire della Città.* The book begins with these words: "It is a cliché to consider negatively the structural changes in the

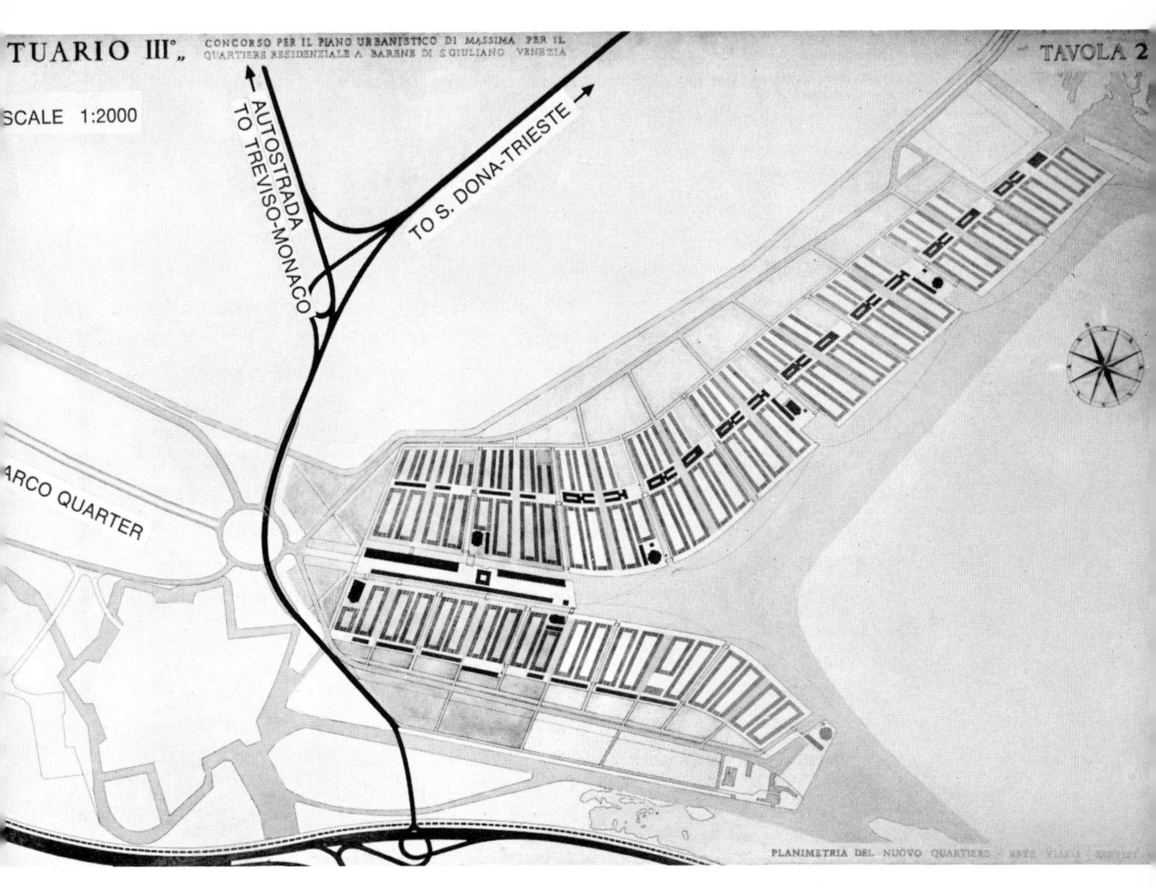

70. *Saverio Muratori and others: Competition for the C.E.P. quarter at the Barene di S. Giuliano, Mestre-Venice, 1959, plan.*

human environment which have arisen out of urbanism." The book is a passionate defense of the advantages of the big city and attacks sociological-urbanistic theories of community, the Mumfordian neighborhood unit, as well as the overevaluation of the garden city tradition subsidized and supported by the building industry. This was the major commitment of the urbanist forces between the first and second periods of I.N.A. Casa and contributed largely to the failure of the supporters of the mass environment.

In the same year, 1959, a national competition was announced for the C.E.P. (Coordinamento Edilizia Populare) neighborhood at Barene di San Giuliano, near Venice. The results showed an extreme radicalism. On the one hand, there was the proposal of Saverio Muratori (*Fig. 70*), whose new project carried out the results of a study on conservation of the historical structure of Venice and, on the other hand, the impressive plan of the Ludovico Quaroni group (*Fig. 71*), which proposed a definite forward step for the solution of the relationships between the urban environment and architectural scale through the placement of great buildngs whose form and dimension depend essentially on their function in the quarter's general form and appearance.

The following year, at the Triennale in Milan, a project for the resettling of the Scalo Farini in the peripheral zone of Milan was proposed, along with a study of suburban areas (*Fig. 72*). This plan—which was influenced by recent British planning—was published in *Casabella* and indicated a clear shift of interest toward the problems of the city and large-scale projects. This change in *Casabella*'s viewpoint reached its climax with the publication of a special issue in May, 1961, which included a critical summary of the last fifteen years of Italian architecture.

Also in 1959, two elements gave Italian culture a new impetus toward these same problems: the discussion of city structure and design became the focus of attention at the meeting of the I.N.U. (National Institute of Urbanism) in Lecce; since its 1957 meeting in Lucca, I.N.U. had moved from the problems of the historical centers to the urban problem in its totality. Moreover, the S.A.U. (Society of Architecture and Urban Studies) was officially founded by a group of Roman architects who had been discussing urban problems for the past three years. S.A.U.'s policy is in direct opposition to the attitudes of the neorealists, a return to the rationalist tradition, and a concern for urbanism as an administrative and political problem. There is also some local effort toward the unrealized industrialization of Rome, toward the necessity for finding a medium of communication comparable to that of *Casabella* in Milan, and toward establishing cultural groups in opposition to I.N.A.R.C.H. (National Institute of Architecture), through which Bruno Zevi had hoped to open a dialogue between architects and the building industry, a plan which ended only in compromise.

Architecturally, the position held by S.A.U. made itself evident

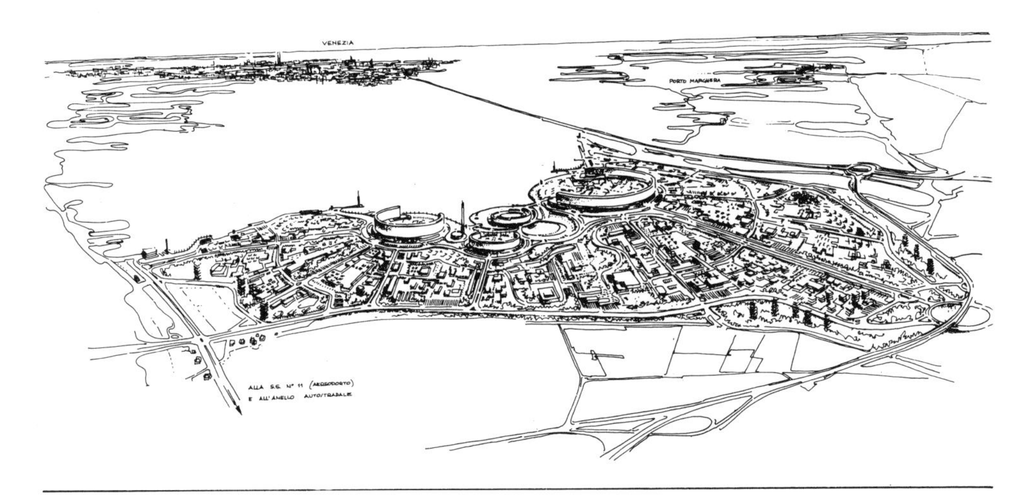

71. *Ludovico Quaroni, Massimo Boschetti, Adolfo de Carlo, Gabriella Esposito, Luciano Giovannini, Aldo Livadiotti, Luciana Menozzi, Alberto Polizzi, Ted Musho: Competition for the C.E.P. quarter at the Barene di S. Giuliano, Mestre-Venice, 1959, drawing.*

72. *Giuan Ugo Polesello, Aldo Rossi, Francesco Tentori: Renewal of the Via Scalo Farini, 12th Triennale, Milan, 1960.*

in the competiton for the Rome Library (1959), and in subsequent attempts at establishing a formal neorationalism. Its most remarkable product was *Le Origni dell'Urbanistica Moderna* (1963) by Leonardo Benevolo, who supported the antiartistic sociological-political interpretation of the development of modern architecture.

The objective urban dialogue seems not only to deprive the structural building dimension of architecture of its meaning, but also to weaken the formally creative substance of architecture. Magazines (especially *Casabella*) stopped considering those problems and limited their reports on architecture. Arguments came to a climax three years later in the competition for the administrative center in Turin (1962; *Figs. 73–74*) which was won by Quaroni. The idea of such a structure as the central business district of the city and as a medium for changing the entire urban equilibrium had already been exemplified in three important, if not wholly fortunate, examples: the administrative center of Milan (the most uninteresting of the three), which was set forth as an elaborate executive design for central town planning; the Florentine project for the Prenestino administrative center in Rome (see *Fig. 34*); and the competition won by Giancarlo De Carlo for the administrative center in Padua.

"The competitors," wrote Paolo Ceccarelli in *Casabella* (Number 278, 1963) in an article entitled "Affluent Urbanism" which dealt with the project for the administrative center of Turin, "insist on the need for assigning precise representative and symbolic values to the Center." The formulation of such values through more or less limited motivations gave an accurate picture of the problem of the architectural-urban relationships and of the fundamental methodological premises involved. The undisputably clear outcome was a sharp division between claims and results, as though theories and intentions were inadequate to formal execution.

After three years of substantially antiformalistic debates, architectural form as a meaningful quality and not only as the medium for a message again became the focus of attention. This process is related in the issue of *Edilizia Moderna* (Number 82/83) which covers Italian architecture up to 1963. "The pattern that we followed," says the introduction, "in the choice of this material led us to consider essentially two parameters: composition not only as an operating process, but above all as the first commitment of architects to reality, and the concept of the formal problem as the structural form of the architectural process."

As a whole, then, this position was characterized by a new interest in an international language, by the experiments in the visual arts of the figurative avant-garde, a belligerence which is sometimes excessively exuberant. The concept of history itself is changed; prehistory and anthropology become a matter of passionate concern to architects. Moreover, there is a new concern with space, with volume which involved a relative insensitivity to details. It affirmed, more-

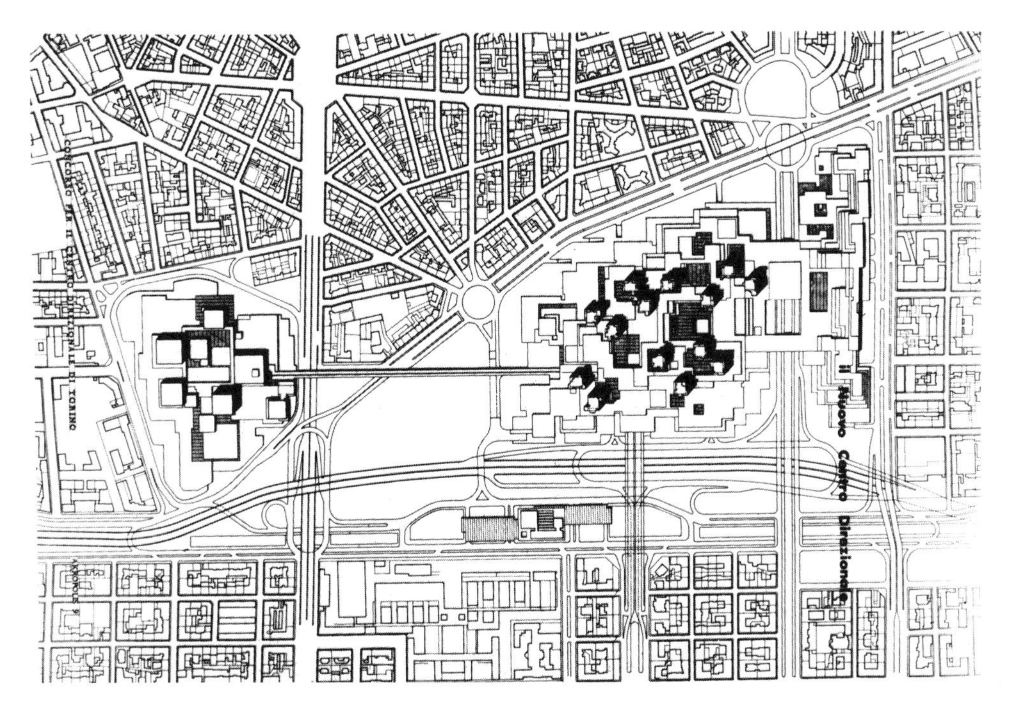

73. *Ludovico Quaroni, Mario Bianco, Gabriella Esposito, Roberto Maestro, Sergio Nicola, Antonio Quistella, Nello Renacco, Aldo Rizzotti, Sugusto Romano: Competition for administration center, Turin, 1962, plan.*

74. *Michele Achilli, Guido Canella, Lucio D'Angiolini, Virgilio Vercelloni: Competition for administration center, Turin, 1962, model.*

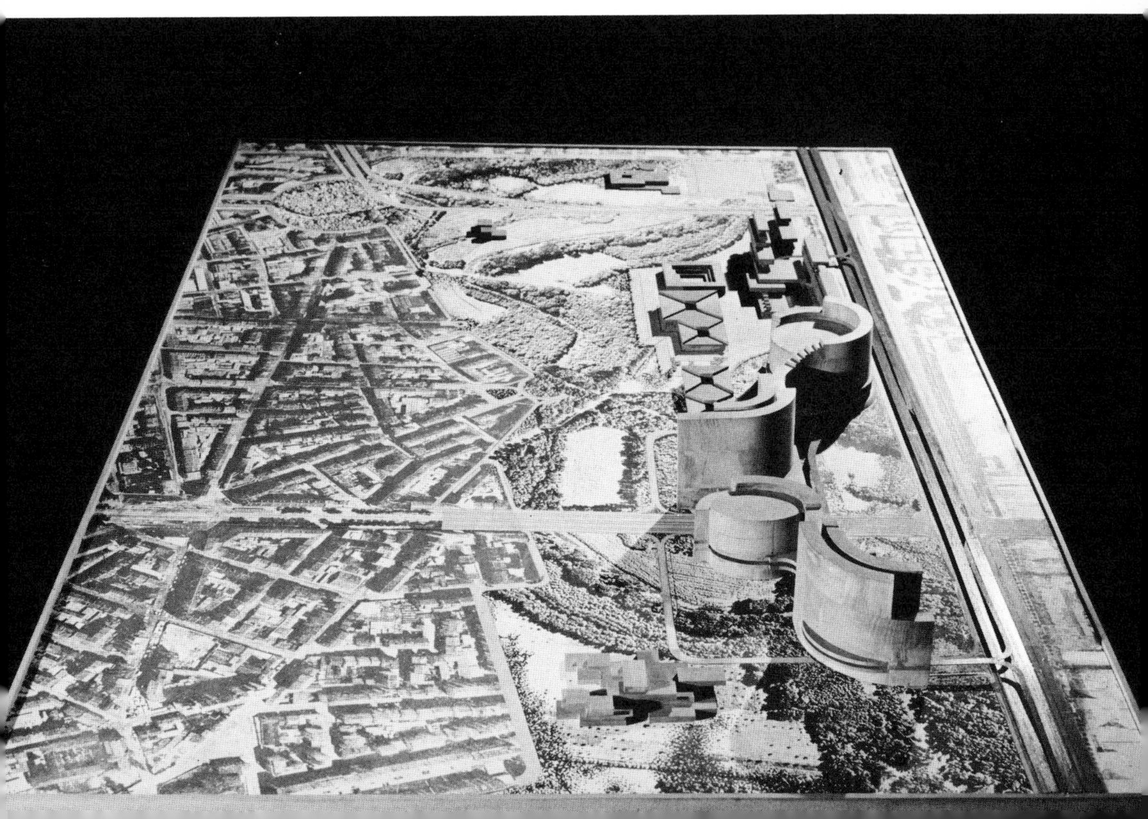

over, a new linguistic engagement, which seemed to be the instrument of a reaction against neorealism, proving the authenticity of its vocation (which was also political) directly through the language of the work itself.

Two artists, who were not very prolific as architects, deserve the credit for this situation; Carlo Scarpa and Ettore Sottssas, Jr. These names considered together will surprise many Italians. But they share, above all, a faith in achieving coherent contact with the world through architecture, and in doing one thing at least very well; this is very important, especially in a country such as Italy, where everyone turns his hand to everything. They both worked in the field of design, handicrafts, interior decoration, and architecture, establishing a coherent connection between these different activities. Both are deeply involved in the recent developments of modern art, but both also have a lasting connection with Viennese culture.

Scarpa has been active over the past years in reestablishing museums—the Albatelli Palace in Palermo, the Palazzo Vecchio in Florence, the Castelvecchio Museum in Verona, the Querini Museum in Venice, the Venezuelan pavilion at Venice's 24th Biennale (*Fig.* 75)—and his work, together with the work of Franco Albini, is appreciated all over the world. He has built only a few buildings and stores, but they convey an extraordinary sense of invention, of imaginative mechanics, of concentration of spatial tension—they are a precious education. Many Venetian architects were among his pupils; he taught Marcello D'Olivo (*Fig. 76*); he taught Gino Valle, from Udine, who is among the most brilliant Italian architects of those in their forties. Valle has been able to incorporate the sense of detail in Scarpa's teaching in visually and technically very advanced works (*Fig. 77*).

Sottssas was largely a designer by training. However, through classical and artistic background (he is also a painter), his understanding of everything human, his passion for the East, his deep love and hatred for American civilization, his deep feelings for a new idea of religion, have prevented him from becoming totally reconciled to technology. He has withdrawn from the world of cultural styles and built up his own world as a coherent tension between a variety of fragments, and as a coordinated sequence (*Fig. 78*).

The only important representative of the new experimental avant-garde in Rome is Maurizio Sacripanti, who has produced a series of projects which are utopic, yet concretely architectural, and which propose an exterior development in the tradition of the new (*Fig. 79*).

The best-known new Florentine architectural work is the Autostrada church by Giovanni Michelucci (*Fig. 80*); many currents merged in this ingenious building, from Hans Scharoun to Le Corbusier (the first for his broad-minded plastic invention, the second for his attempt to re-create in architecture the experience of in-

75. *Carlo Scarpa: Venezuela pavilion, 24th Biennale, Venice, 1956.*

76. *Marcello d'Olivo and Vincenzo Simonitti: Hotel, Manacore, Gargano, 1962.*

77. *Gino Valle: Building for electrical household appliances, Pordenone, 1963, facade.*

78. *Ettore Sottsass, Jr.: Main entrance, 12th Triennale, Milan, 1960.*

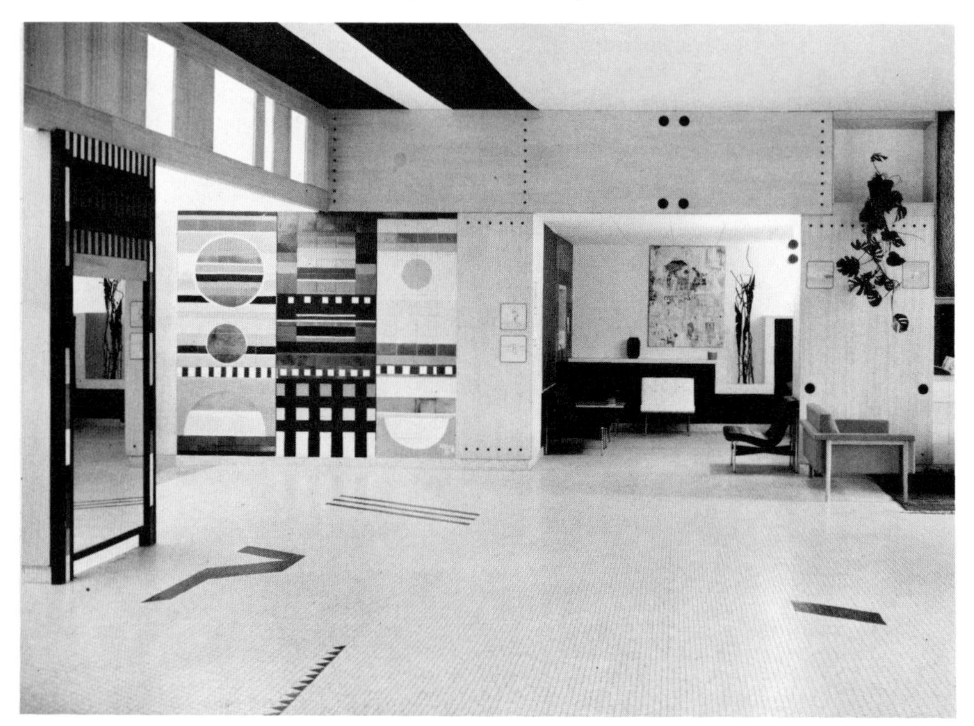

79. *Maurizio Sacripanti: Competition for a museum, Padua, 1967.*

80. *Giovanni Michelucci: Church of S. Giovanni, Autostrada del Sole, Florence, 1962.*

formal painting, as in the tentlike covering), as well as the ignorant, presumptuous, and degenerate craftsmanship so widespread today in Tuscany. Leonardo Savioli's and Leonardo Ricci's buildings (*Figs. 81–82*) should also be considered as experimental works, and the young Florentine generation of architects share their point of view.

How much is left of the first generation of Italian rationalism, and how much thrives in the new situation? Not too much, regrettably. Albini, B.P.R., Gardella, Mollino, Ridolfi and others once produced outstanding works, perhaps the most mature products of the era, but their impetus is no longer the same. We give them the credit that is due masters, but homage given this sort of man represents at the same time an alienation from reality. (This is not to pass judgment on them, since reality is not a value *per se*, but it is simply a statement of fact.) Against their will, many of them have generously accepted responsibilities in the schools, which take a great deal of their energies, or they have exposed their theses in public debates (for example, the one organized by Samonà on the regional plan of the Trentino and the reconstruction of Vajont), and they have often been the target of unjust and ungenerous criticism. Samonà for instance, was criticized for taking advantage of a natural disaster (the breaking of a dam and the destruction of a village) to further his own theories on urbanism. Their cultural point of view is symbolized by their interest in design, an interest generally shared by the following, middle generation. For this reason the Triennale, after its eighth exhi-

81. *Leonardo Savioli, Marci Dezzi Bardeschi, Vittorio Giorgini, Giuseppe Gori, and Danilo Santi: Popular buildings at C.E.P., Sorgane (Florence).*

82. *Leonardo Ricci: Villaggio Monte degli Ulivi church, Riesi, Sicily, 1966, drawing.*

bition in 1947, was in their hands and only the thirteenth Triennale (1963) evidenced some new directions.

The younger generation, those who first experimented during the period of striving for reality, followed. Almost all of them were committed to positions in the schools, influenced by criticism, and not sufficiently committed to their profession. They produced very few, albeit significant, works following the monumental projects of Aldo Rossi (*Fig. 83*), and at the thirteenth Triennale, there were competitions by Carlo Aymonino (*Fig. 84*), some new work by the architects of Turin—Roberto Gabetti and Aimaro D'Isola (*Fig. 85*), Piero De Rossi, Elio Luzi and Sergio Zaretti (*Fig. 86*), Giorgio Raineri (*Fig. 87*) and the daring neoeclectic city hall by Michele Achilli, Daniele Brigidini, Guido Canella, and Laura Lazzari (*Fig. 88*). Then came those for whom all this was mostly an intellectual adventure, and who slowly returned to architecture through their interest in

83. *Aldo Rossi: Arcades of Parma and the monument of Segrate, studies.*

84. *Carlo Aymonino: Concorse, reconstruction of the Teatro Paganini, Parma.*

85. *Aimaro Oreglia D'Isola, Augusto Cavallari, Roberto Gabetti, Giorgio Raineri, Murat: High school, Vallette quarter, Turin, 1964.*

urban and regional planning, bringing with them a group of new materials and new problems, often partially concealed by unimportant experiments, too small for their underlying concept or expressed through designs shamefully disguised under the label of research.

By accepting architecture as a fact of significative communication, or a formal linguistic fact, architects affirm their own subjectivity. Although the architects' increased freedom of action has enlarged the possibilties of architecture, the architects must carefully choose those liberties which will stimulate these possibilities. This assumption of responsibility on a formal level, this meeting the world head on—these enabled the younger architects to enlarge and strengthen their work.

Now the task is to move beyond the mere assertion of experimental attitudes, for the intention to invert ideology and language thus supports the creative process's role as an instrument for liberation from the feeling of impotence, and as a legitimate process of invention, without ignoring those precious elements of action, complexity and ambiguity. We are now left with the problem of judging whether the reality that experiments have built up is progressing or regressing, and whether reality produces possibilities or uselessly obstructs the development of the world.

86. *Piero de Rossi, Sergio Zaretti, and Elio Luzi: Towers, Viale Pitagora, Turin, 1964.*

87. *Giorgio Raineri: Noviziato delle Suore di Carità, Turin, 1965.*

88. *Michele Achilli, Daniele Brigidini, Guido Canella, Laura Lazzari: City hall, Segrate, Milan, 1965.*

THE ROLE OF INDUSTRIAL DESIGN

IT may seem strange to discuss industrial design in an essay on architecture; however, there are clear historical reasons for considering design as part of the culture and the history of modern Italian architecture. This is because design originates and develops within the tradition of the applied arts. The designers come from widespread and often unconnected professions and are trained empirically but have come to industrial design because of its connection with an unsettled industrial situation whose tradition is more recent than the tradition of other European countries.

Almost all historians and critics agree that Italian design as a clearly characterized phenomenon can only be considered after 1945. Before then, and before the Second World War, Italian design experiments were rare and confined mainly to the house and home furnishings. There were a few exceptions: the experiments of Giuseppe Pagano, the design for the E.T.R.-200 locomotive, the teamwork of Adriano Olivetti and Marcello Nizzoli in typewriter design begun in 1936 (*Fig. 89*), the first radios designed by L. Caccia Dominioni and Livio and Pier Castiglioni (*Fig. 90*) and shown at the sixth Triennale (earlier examples were too tied to interior decoration to be considered pure design), and finally some purely industrial design, such as the body of the Lancia Aprilia automobile in 1937 (*Fig. 91*). These are the only cases in which one can talk of the attempt to control the structure and form of the object in the sense of modern design. Everything accomplished before the war was principally connected with attempts at prefabrication and rationalization, or to experimental works prepared for special exhibitions; often, for the Triennale, artists concentrated on shifting the design of furniture away from craft tradition toward a real modern renewal.

Mention has already been made of the work of Gio Ponti at the Triennale, which sought to renew the Italian handicraft tradition. Mention must again be made of Franco Albini, whose knowledge and energy contributed greatly to the experiments in contemporary Italian furniture (*Fig. 92*), and a few examples of such energy also appear in the works of Edoardo Persico, as well as some furniture by Gigi Chessa and Alberto Sartoris.

In 1945, cultural conditions which had stirred up the arguments about modern architecture and creative design in Italy were totally changed. Just as fascism and war had brought a whole vein of *belles-lettres* to an end, as we have seen, so these events also ended the

89. *Marcello Nizzoli: Olivetti typewriter Lexikon 80, 1946.*

90. *L. Caccia Dominioni, Livio and Pier Giacomo Castiglioni: Plastic radio receiver Phonola, 1938.*

91. *Lancia Aprilia automobile with self-supporting body, 1937.*

stylistic polemics of rationalism in architecture, replacing them with a cultural issue with realistic implications. Design, however, was seen by many as an agency of "major" culture: both as being an ally of capitalist production and as being an evasion of the "realist" movements of the time. From its start, modern production more or less consciously set out to elevate the problem of design, introducing it as an integral part of the productive cycle.

Between 1945 and 1951, Italian design developed along two comparatively independent lines. First, the heritage of the rationalist culture asserted itself through some objects of exceptional value (the Lexicon 80 and Lettera 22 Olivetti typewriters designed by Nizzoli), which were a definite step forward toward the creation of a rapport between mechanism and body, following a ten-year-old tradition, or with the sports car designed by Zavanella in 1948, or the first group of furniture designed by Franco Albini (*Fig. 93*). Second, industry almost spontaneously produced some pieces of remarkable formal interest (such as the activity of Pinin Farina, *Fig. 94*) and expanded its areas of concern (such as the scooter in 1948, the Vespa Piaggio in the same year, and the Lambretta Innocenti in 1949, as well as the small Isetta automobile in 1953, *Fig. 95*).

92. *Franco Albini and Franca Helg: Malacca and bamboo-cane armchair Margherita, 1950.*

93. *Franco Albini: Dining room furniture, Ferrarin home, 1932.*

94. *Automobile Cisitalia, Turin: Cisitalia automobile, 1940. Body on a tubular frame by Pinin Farina.*

95. *Small automobile Isetta, 1953.*

Between 1951 and 1957, two important phenomena occurred in Italy. On the one hand, design became organized on a cultural level. The ninth, tenth, and eleventh Triennales devoted important exhibitions to design, and this mood permeated the entire exhibitions. At the tenth Triennale (1954), an international meeting on design was organized, which had great theoretical importance. Many international designers, theorists, and critics participated in discussions centering around the methods and meaning of design. The magazine *Stile Industria* was founded, and under Alberto Rosselli's direction fifteen issues were published up to 1962; in 1956, A.D.I. (Associazione Disegno industriale) was founded in Milan, the industrial center of Italy, and the city where the most important designers, experts, and theoreticians of the graphic arts are working even today. Finally, in 1958 La Rinascente, a large department store, established the Premio Compasso d'Oro for Italian design, the most important goal of which was to introduce the concept of design to industrial groups.

On the other hand, a closer and more steady cooperation between firms and designers began, although at first it was very limited and often only on the promotional level. The Necchi sewing machines of Marcello Nizzoli; the Arflex foam rubber furniture of Marco Zanuso (*Fig. 96*); Arteluce, with many designers; electric watches by B.P.R.; followed by Michele Provinciali, Gino Valle (watches), Borletti and Zanuso (sewing machines), Richard Ginori and Gariboldi (ceramics).

96. *Marco Zanuso: Armchair Lady, 1950.*

Between 1957 and 1960, the most interesting Italian phenomenon was a return to history and artisan tradition, similar to what was taking place in architecture. Theoretical as well as design innovations marked the most interesting furniture; objects which were controversial or challenging in themselves were generally produced by the younger generation. The most significant exhibition (which, in a deformative sense, goes back to themes initiated in the furniture designs of Ignazio Gardella, L. Caccia Dominioni, and Franco Albini), "New Designs for Italian Furniture," saw the beginning of the movement later to be called neo-Liberty.

After 1960, spurred by the growth in consumer buying over the previous years, the field of the designer broadened. Design gained a new importance through its connection with business, on the one hand, and its connection with the methodological organization of planning on the other hand. Design also became one of the issues involved in prefabrication and industrialization of building, both as to methods (see Gino Valle [*Fig. 97*] and Angelo Mangiarotti [*Fig. 98*] with reinforced concrete, Mario Bellini and Feal with Claudio Conte's prefabricated metal, Leonardo Fiori with wood, Silvano Zorzi [*Fig. 99*], Pier Luigi Nervi, and Riccardo Morandi with the assemblage system in concrete), and as to improvement of design, along with the coordination of the elements of construction.

At the opposite pole, design moved toward the visual arts, toward the formal experiments based for the most part on specific and refined craft traditions, to the transformation of objects into symbols; this contrasted to the attempts at using industrial methods and industrial processes to create new visual or plastic objects, superimposing and combining sculpture, painting, design and environment.

In the past few years, Italy has also tried to organize a school of industrial design by converting art institutes into schools of design (at Venice, Florence, and Rome), and by introducing the designer into the administration of industrial corporations. The most avant-garde examples were supplied by the teamwork of Adriano Olivetti and Ettore Sottsass, Jr. (*Fig. 100*) in the field of electromechanics, electronics, and small computers.

Italian design over these past years has won a great international reputation. English products offered a balance between needs and solutions; American products were above all designed to take advantage of the highly developed technology and well-established production system; French products had the benefit of the rapport between the engineering and production fields, based on efficient mechanical and engineering innovations. As for Italian design, it was above all found to be capable of making up for deficiencies in production and marketing, which were still considerable, and of consumption, while growing on the technological organization level and improvised on the methodological level, by means of brilliant, aesthetic solutions to specific problems.

97. *Gino Valle: Cement prefabricated panels, 1963.*

98. *Angelo Mangiarotti, Emag plant, Monza, Milan, 1966.*

99. *Silvano Zorzi: thin plate lining of the canal of the Pontecorvo Plant.*

The international effects of Italian design are mainly the result of its experimental and pioneering industrial activity. Very often industry gives a secondary and improvisational importance to design; at other times it gives design the total responsibility for characterizing the product. Taken as a whole, this situation offers an opportunity for operating within a defined area, giving greater freedom of action. The situation has changed over the years because of the enlarged and stabilized cooperation between the designer, industry and distribution, and because of the increased opportunity for the professional designer to act in an autonomous manner, and to use his methods for furthering the unity of general design principles, which aim for the formal structurizing of the entire physical environment of man's activity. Methodology becomes more and more specialized as it seeks a rapport among the areas of function, design and typology, production and technology, and distribution and consumption of the specific product.

It is interesting to note that critical interest in this field is waning. From Guilio Carlo Argan to Gillo Dorfles to the special issue of *Edilizia Moderna* (Number 85) which was dedicated to "design," it is easy to discern the shift of interest from the classical thesis of the construction of an object and the social meaning of this operation to the problems of distribution and consumption which are given prime importance by the consumer, not only from an ideological point of view, but in the field of formal and functional relationships and communications.

100. *Ettore Sottsass, Jr., Olivetti computer Logos 27-2, 1965.*

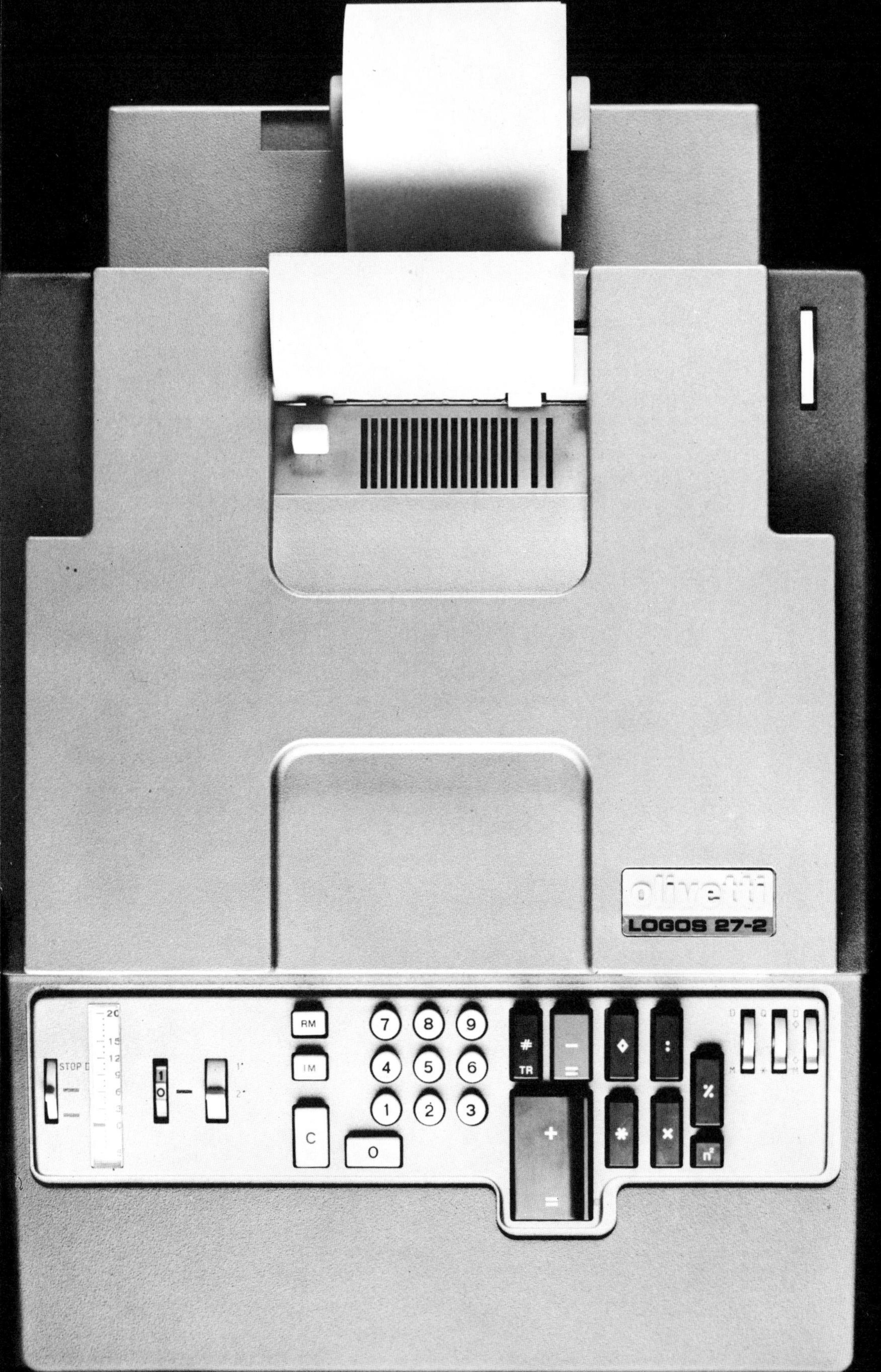
olivetti
LOGOS 27-2
RM
IM
C
TR
STOP

THE REVOLT IN THE SCHOOLS OF ARCHITECTURE

THE main subject of this final chapter is the problems of the architecture schools. There is good reason to do so. First, the schools of architecture have appointed themselves as a privileged arena for architectural debate. No longer are magazines or pressure groups the centers of activity; the schools are now the area where the discussion and planning of Italian architecture laboriously takes place. Second, by the problems imposed by mass education and by the idea of student research, future work may take the form of a radical alternative to contemporary methods of architectural planning and design.

It has been obvious for many years that the traditional position of the architectural profession in Italy has been changing. It is obvious that problems of national interest should be faced by the public cultural organizations, such as universities. Moreover, schools are beginning to organize their own critical publications as an alternative to the publishing field. It should be added that up to now there is neither a planning school nor a school of industrial design in Italy, and that the entire training for management and for engineering in the building industry is sporadic and far below university level. We cannot analyze these categories by themselves as we analyze architecture—even if we acknowledge them as isolated problems in the progress of the building industry. The study of planning experiments has so far been strictly confined to public or private study centers. As we have noted, Italian design is still an isolated cultural event in a pioneering stage, consisting of associations and groups, while technological organization has reached its highest point of progress on the "consultation" level, where planning is organized on an interdisciplinary and rigorously productivist level.

The forces of renewal characteristic of the different schools of architecture strongly emphasize, at the expense of standards of professional efficiency and techniques, theoretical and utopian aspects with strong morphological and sociopolitical orientation rather than a technical and constructional outlook. This brings into question the value of the architectural discipline, and the preservation of that discipline.

It would seem that the questions, "Who is the architect?" and "What is his place in society?" characteristic of the striving for reality movement, has been replaced by the question, "What is architecture, what does it consist of, what are its problems, and what are

101. *Students of Carlo Aymonimo: Administration center of Centocelle, Rome, 1963, plan. Architectural Composition course project, University of Rome.*

its social proposals and social challenges?" All this furthers the anti-ideological and antideductive movement which has arisen out of the crises of the 1960's and which seems to be directed toward the search for an objectivity which cannot be called scientific, but which can certainly be considered as an attempt to make communicable the subjective operation by which architectural language as a means of communication is constructed.

Three spheres of interest can easily be distinguished in the architecture schools. The first deals with the notion of the city as an artifact and tends to return to architecture its "monumental" meaning. The second tends to investigate the notion of physical environment, and, starting from the idea of formal or functional relationships and materials, attempts to establish a new way of adapting to all dimensional scales. The third, under the influence of American theory, tends to direct its interests toward formalizing the project procedures, replacing the old material technology with project technology.

The first category (principally applied to Milan, Venice, and Rome) focuses mainly on the relationship between typology and urban morphology; through the idea of typology and its renewal, it tends to unite the different functional and dimensional levels, while producing inequalities of meaning within a limited physical environment (*Fig. 101*); the idea is therefore to concentrate the civil meaning of public services linked to certain infrastructural ties, at the cost of leaving to production and consumption logic the other problem areas such as, for example, the problem of residence. This tendency makes assumptions based on the idea of originality, beginning with ideas of multifunctional buildings and the conglomeration of services and experiments in new languages. A second pole of the same tendency is the idea of architecture as testimony, durability, and monumentality (which linked the neoclassical architects of the French Revolution with Adolf Loos and Le Corbusier, and some aspects of the work of German rationalists such as Hannes Mayer and Albert Klein, culminating with Louis Kahn) (*Fig. 102*).

Adherents of both of these cultural aspects consider architecture as monument and emphasize its monumental aspect as a cultural and ideological medium for becoming aware of the world. They see architecture as being made up of rigidly classifiable matters and objects (the building industry identifying with the German positivism and French rationalist ideal).

Due to its narrow and antitechnological method, that point of view has often been considered antimodern in the formal sphere, especially by those who do not agree with the strong idealization to which it gives rise. Similarly, the outlook of those who put forward the concept of environment as the essence of architecture is said to negate the validity of the discipline. Supporters of these two attitudes are accused for their excessive interest in form and history, for considering the accumulated past as a rich source for architec-

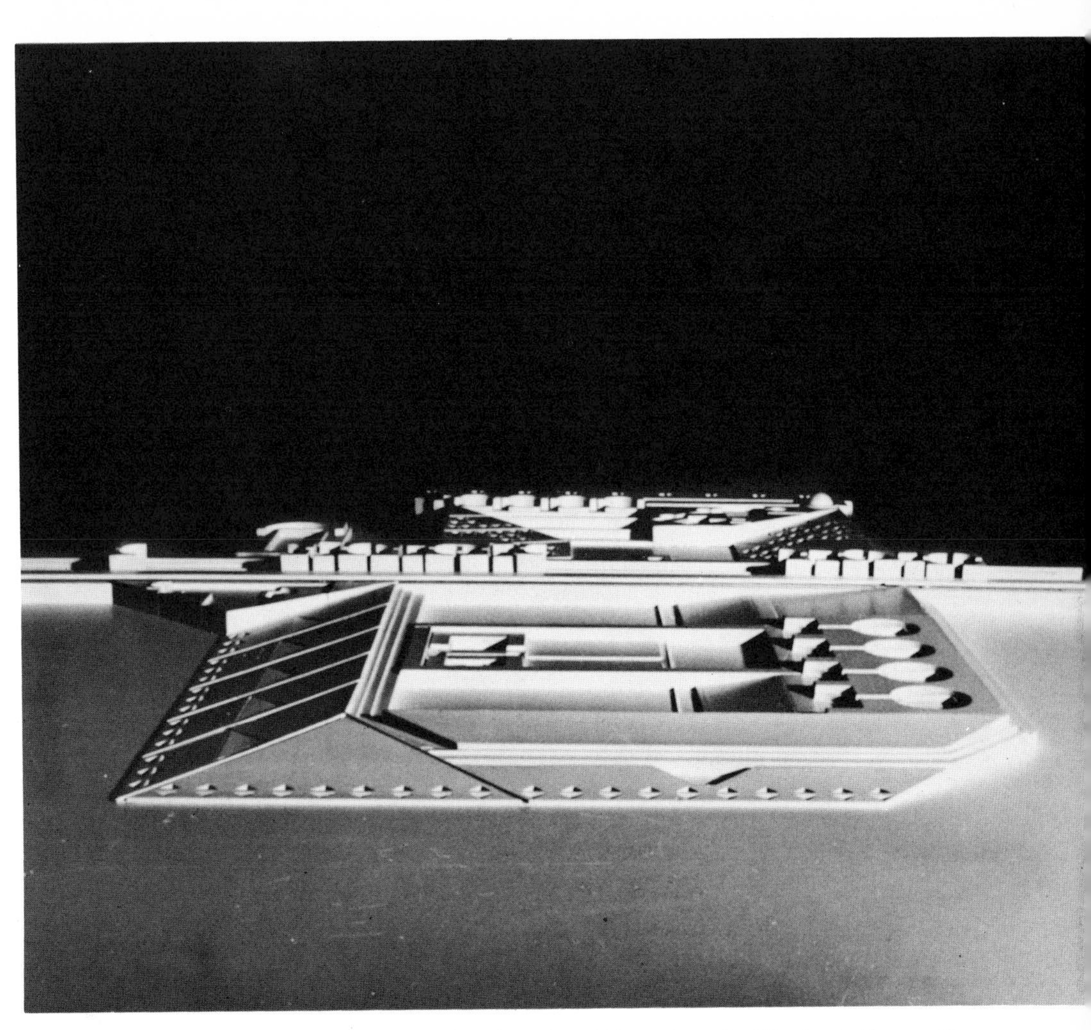

102. *Students of Ludovico Quaroni: A university city, 1967, plan. Architectural Composition course project, University of Rome.*

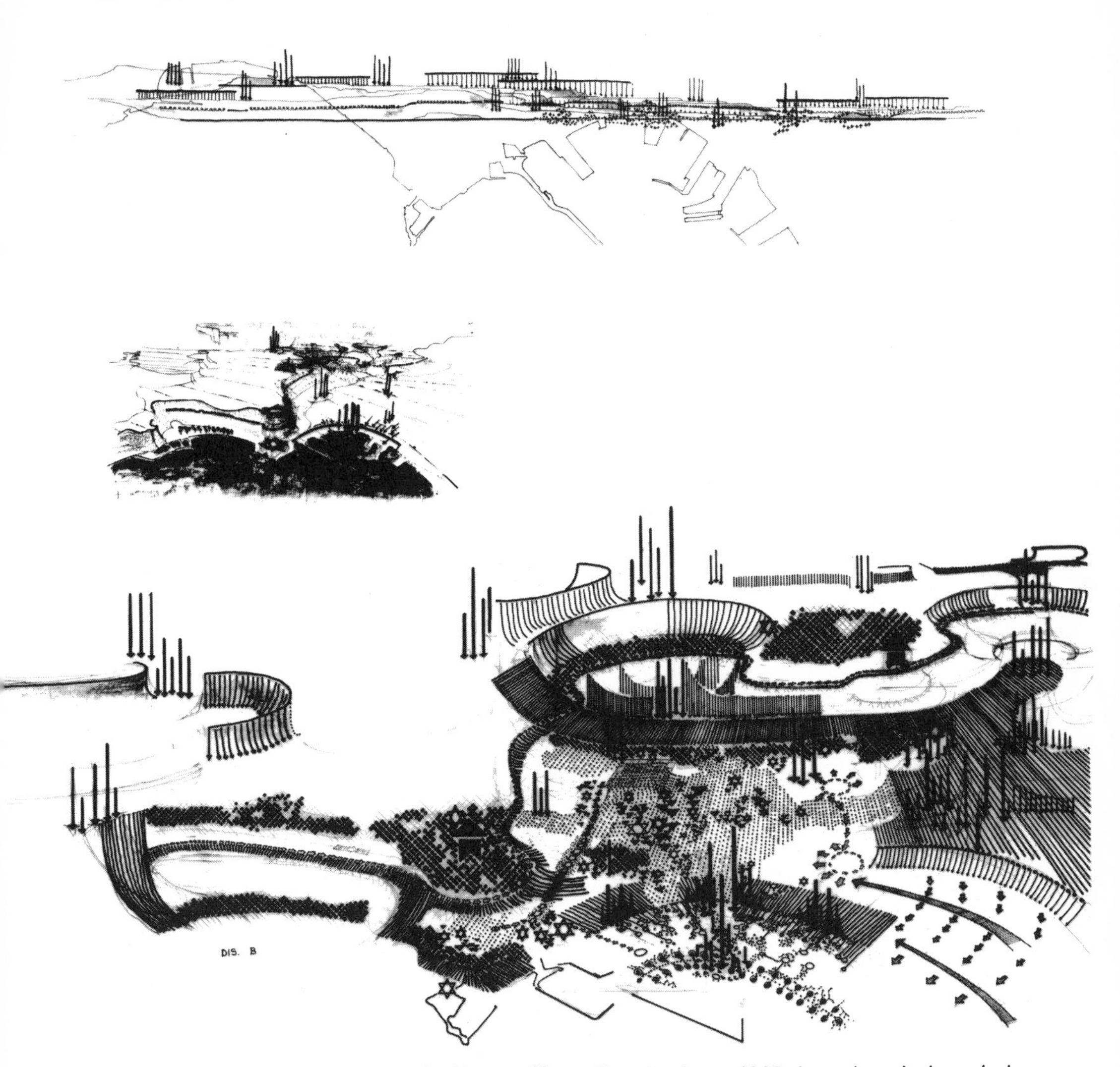

104. *Salvatore Bisogni and Antonio Renna: Neapolitan territory, 1965, formal analysis and plan for transformation.*

103. *Cesare Pellegrini: Facilities for a vacation at Linate, Milan, 1963, project.*

ture and as a dimension of reality. Moreover, both are accused of making practical conditions abstract, mainly by those who confuse reality and theory and who are unwilling to acknowledge the role played by research in architecture. The second attitude, that which is concerned primarily with physical environment, gives great emphasis to the idea of the mobility and ambiguity of meaning and an enlargement of the significant content of architecture.

Architecture seems to be increasingly sensitive to the theory of communication, to the most recent experiments in the figurative

105. *Students of Vittorio Gregotti: Analysis and plan for transformation of the northern Milanese territory, 1966. Architectural Elements course project, Politecnico, Milan.*

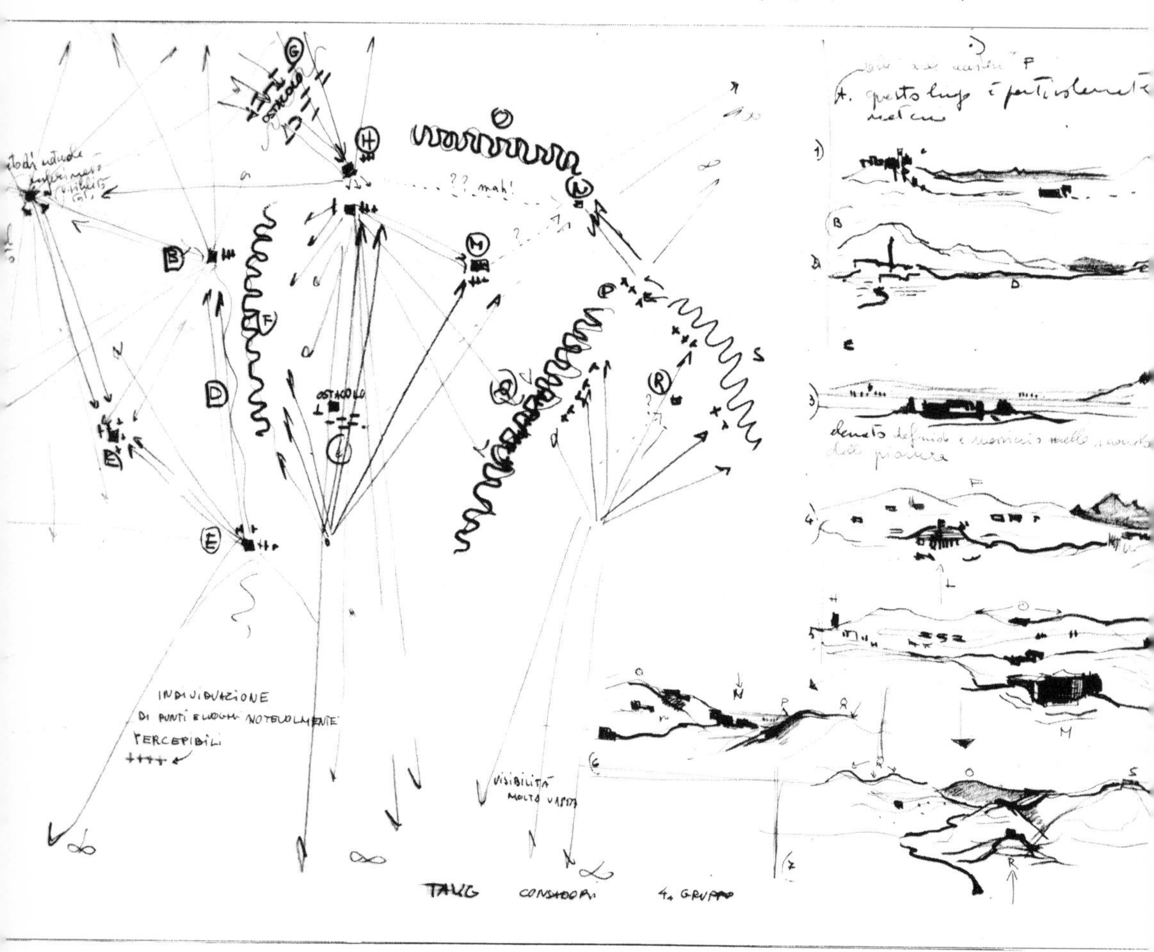

arts, especially the artists not connected with geometrical abstraction and to ties with other expressive forms, without repudiating the specific constructional role of architecture (*Fig. 103*). Therefore it does not focus on the problem of the city, notwithstanding the importance given to population density and stratification. Its main effort is devoted to creating environmental systems as special areas, without distinction between natural and artificial environments (*Figs. 104–105*).

Design is connected with distribution and formal or functional

relationships, rather than seen in terms of single objects; architecture is considered more from the point of view of the surroundings and the site than of the space to be filled; the processes of mimesis and collage are employed, and the idea of creativity, of inductive thinking and of complex and stratified order become predominant (*Fig. 106*). Somehow, between these two attitudes, urban structural experiments in Florence—influenced by an *informal* symbolism parallel with movement in painting—have created a sense of impartiality

106. *Franco Purini and Laura Thermes: The Lungoteveri, Rome, 1966, plan for a new structure.*

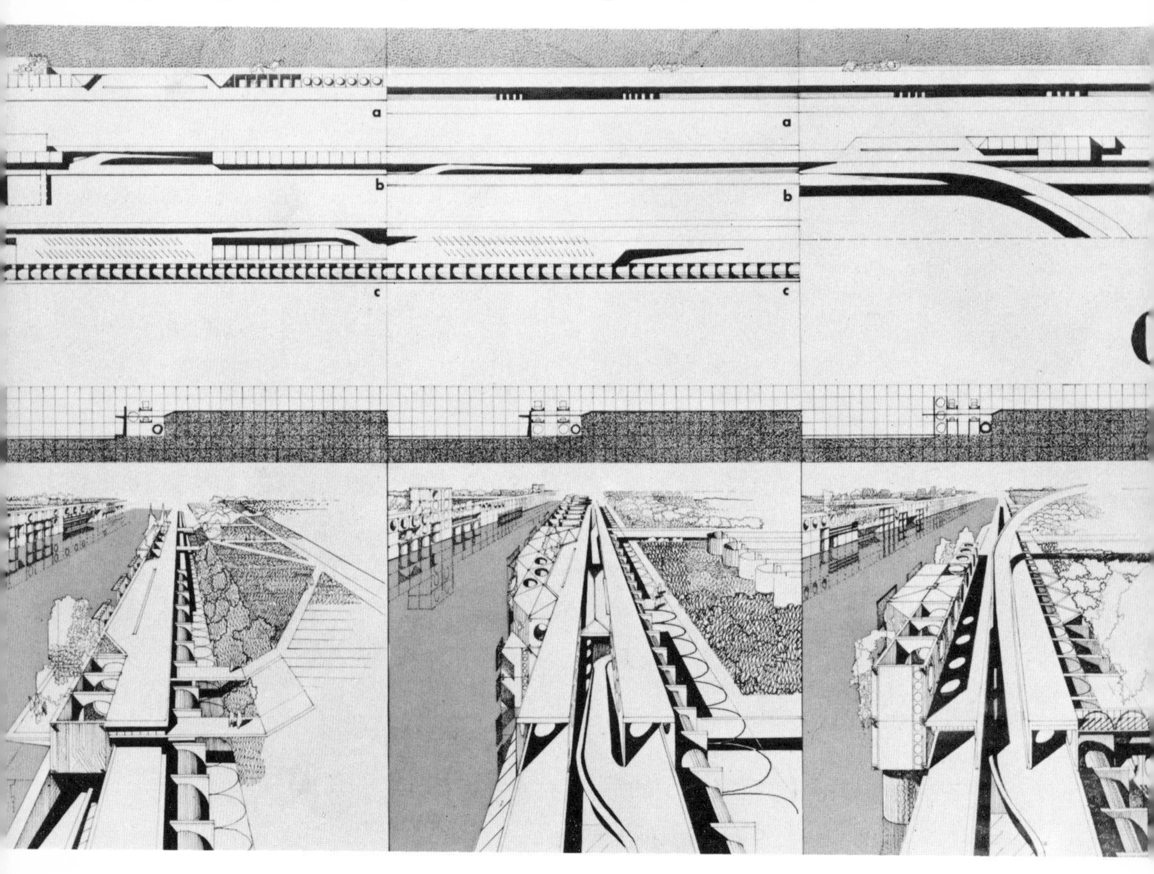

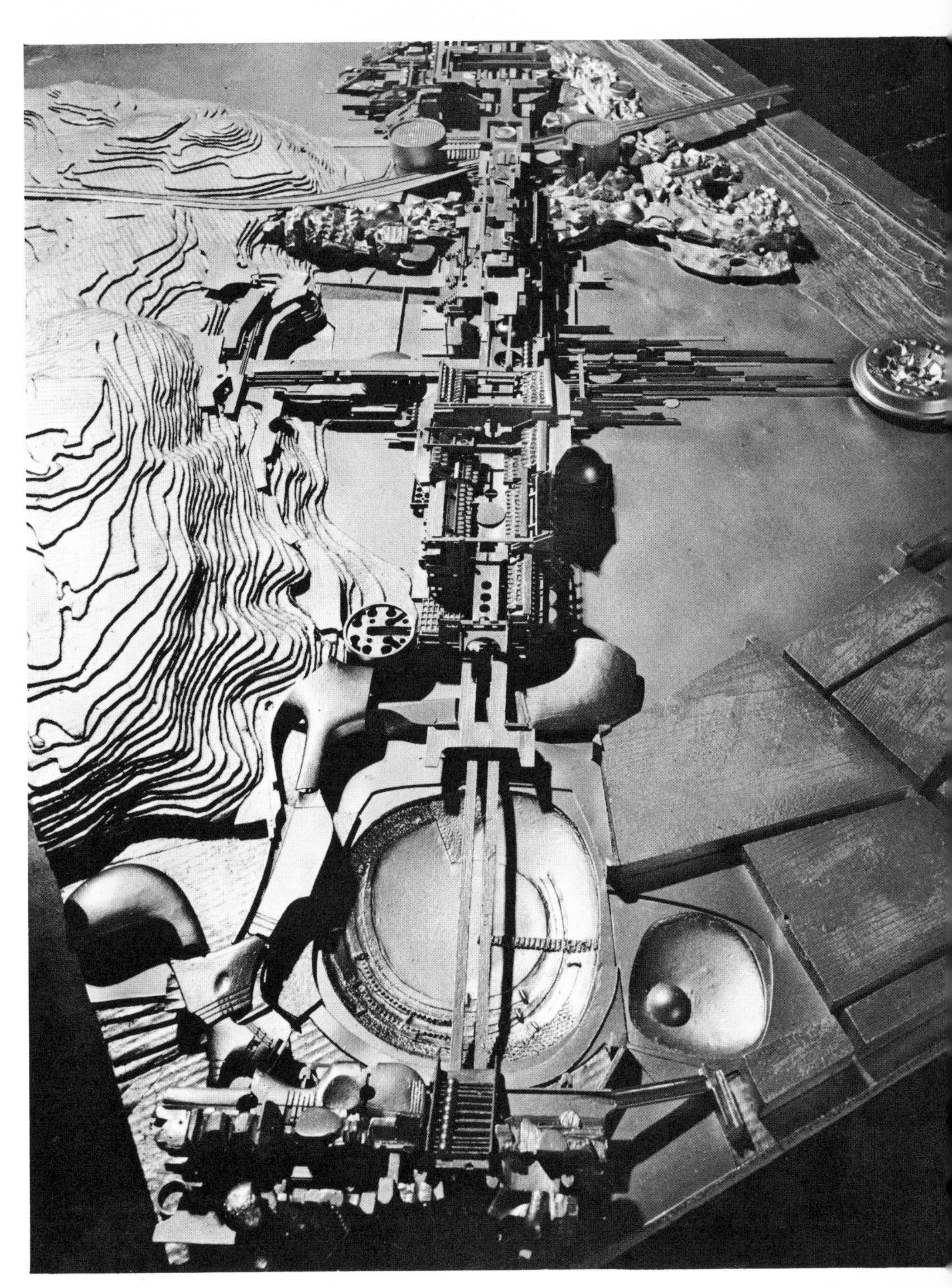

107. *Students of Ludovico Savioli: San Frediano quarter, Florence, 1966, plan for new structure. Course project, University of Florence.*

108. *Ludovico Quaroni, Adolfo de Carlo, Massimo Amodei, Roberto Berardi, Behamin Hagler: Government center, Tunis, 1966, model.*

with regard to materials, and have a direct interest for that city, with its characteristic of collective monumentality (*Fig. 107*). Ludovico Quaroni and his group support and carry on this position, but with greater maturity. The genuine, spontaneous personality of Quaroni is bound up with a poetics of ambiguity and a natural inclination toward eclecticism. His strong feeling of instability attracts him to the notion of environment, but on the other hand, he sees its faults. His attempt, therefore, consists in stabilizing the environmental problems around the idea of city design. His plan for the government center of Tunis seems to materialize architecturally his dialectical ideas, and we accept this plan totally as the embodiment of the most interesting contemporary concerns of tlalian architecture (*Figs. 108–109*). Franco Albini's experiments for the Milan subways are symmetrical examples: they are, to our knowledge, the only Italian examples which use design coherently for constructing a series of environments commissioned by a public agency (*Fig. 110*).

The architectural schools' third sphere of interest is rationalization of the planning and design process, either through expressing or articulating methods. Here the neopositivistic influences of the Ulm school and of recent American methodological experiments, together with the idea of the scientific process, are highly visible.

Is the assertion of this theoretical-utopian outlook a hindrance or an impetus for architectural solutions of building problems? How can professional experience and research be joined when they seem so far apart? It is difficult to answer these questions today. Today's

109. *Government center, Tunis, plan.*

productive politicosocial and cultural situation does not seem near a quick solution in Italy. Once again, we are faced with the creation of a culture on a line whose extremes are, on the one hand, the most refined expression and progressive production, and on the other, the needs of a country torn by internal inequity. Nevertheless, the problem is to keep these dialectics alive and capable of intercommunication, and not to withdraw from present difficulties out of an allegiance to a utopian ideal, not to indulge in current polemics and be overwhelmed by them. This desperate situation, now purely political, is seen today in the universities. In Italy, thousands of students dissent from the elitist class which they feel dissociates itself from social injustice.

This revolutionary movement involves many countries but in Italy has often originated in architectural schools. I believe that at its roots lies a basic problem of architecture: to design or project creatively not only our wealth and our well-being, but also our choice of our own direction—which is not a renunciation of the world, but the affirmation of a world devoted to eliminating repression in ourselves and in the structure of present-day society.

The same notion of needs and services so closely connected with the problems of architecture is the issue at the basis of today's student movements, which seek to understand what is false and what is true in such a situation, to understand the relationship between needs and those desires which, more than reason, form the dynamic element in history.

This transfer of attention from "need" to "desire" according to the French psychoanalyst Jacques Lacan, is not the luxury of a wealthy society, but the hallmark of every society. The goal of architecture as a manufacturer of continuously different and continually new relationships, as the physical structuring of imagination, is indissolubly linked with it.

110. *Franco Albini and Franca Helg (with Antonio Piva and Bob Noorda): Subway, Milan, 1963.*

SELECTIVE BIBLIOGRAPHY

In chronological order

Papini, Roberto. *Le Arti d'Oggi; Architettura e Arti Decorative in Europa.* Milan, 1930.

Piacentini, Marcello. *Architettura d'Oggi.* Rome, 1930.

Fillia, Luigi, ed. *La Nuova Architettura.* Turin, 1931.

Sartoris, Alberto. *Gli Elementi dell'Architettura Funzionale.* Milan, 1932.

Argan, Giulio Carlo, Carlo Levi, Mattero Marangoni *et al. Dopo Sant'Elia.* Milan, 1936.

Pagano, Giuseppe and Guarniero Daniel. *Architettura Rurale Italiana.* Milan, 1936.

Bontempelli, Massimo. *Valori Primordiali.* Rome, 1938.

Pica, Agnoldomenico. *Architettura Moderna in Italia.* Milan, 1941.

Nervi, Pier Luigi. *Scienza o Arte del Costruire?* Rome, 1945.

Zevi, Bruno. *Verso un'Architettura Organica.* Turin, 1945. (*Towards an Organic Architecture.* London, 1950.)

Consiglio Nazionale delle Richerche. *Manuale dell'Architetto.* Rome, 1946.

Labo, Mario. *Giuseppe Terragni*, Milan, 1947.

Diotallevi, Irenio, and Marescotti, Francesco. *Il Problema Sociale, Economico e Construttivo dell'Abitazione.* Milan, 1948.

Zevi, Bruno. *Saper Vedere l'Architettura.* Turin, 1948. *(Architecture as Space; How to Look at Architecture.* New York, 1957.)

Sartoris, Alberto. *Introduzione alla Architettura Moderna.* Milan, 1949.

Zevi, Bruno, *Storia dell'Architettura Moderna.* Turin, 1950.

Argan, Giulio Carlo. *Walter Gropius e la Bauhaus.* Turin, 1951.

Veronesi, Giulia. *Difficoltà Politiche dell 'Architettura in Italia, 1920–1940.* Milan, 1953.

Kidder-Smith, G. E. *L'Italia Costruisce.* Milan, 1955. (*Italy Builds.* New York, 1955.)

Pagani, Carlo. *Architettura Italiana Oggi.* Milan, 1955 (with English text).

Cederna, Antonio. *I Vandali in Casa.* Bari, 1956.

Ciribini, G. *Architettura e Industria.* Milan, 1958.

Rogers, Ernesto N. *Esperienza dell'Architettura.* Turin, 1958.

"L'Architettura Moderna in Italia," *La Casa*, no. 6 (1959).

Pica, Agnoldomenico. *Architettura Italiana Ultima.* Milan, 1959. (*Recent Italian Architecture.* London, 1960).

Samonà, Giuseppe. *L'Urbanistica e l'Avvenire della Città negli Stati Europei.* Bari, 1959.

Aquarone, Alberto. *Grandi Città e Aree Metropolitane in Italia.* Bologna, 1961. "Quindici Anni di Architettura Italiana," *Casabella*, no. 251 (1961).

Sereni, Emilio. *Storia del Paesaggio Agrario Italiano.* Bari, 1961.

Dorfles, Gillo. *Simbolo Comunicazione Consumo.* Turin, 1962.

Insolera, Italo. *Roma Moderna.* Turin, 1962.

Istituto Lombardo Studi Economici e Sociali (I.L.S.E.S.). *Atti del Seminario di Stresa sul Tema: La Nuova Dimensione della Città, La Città Regione.* Milan, 1962.

Aspetti dell' Arte Contemporanea *Catalogo della Mostra dell' Aquila.* Rome, 1963.

Benevolo, Leonardo. *Le Origini dell'Urbanistica Moderna.* Bari, 1963.
Dorfles, Gillo. *Il Disegno Industriale e la Sua Estetica.* Bologna, 1963.
"Architettura Italiana 1963," *Edilizia Moderna*, no. 82/83 (1964).
Aymonino, Carlo, ed. *La Città Territorio, Un Esperimento Didattico sul Centro Direzionale di Centocelle a Rome.* Bari, 1964.
Tafuri, Manfredo. *Ludovico Quaroni.* Milan, 1964.
Veronesi, Giulia, ed. *Tutte le Opere di Persico.* Milan, 1964.
XXX, Utopia della Realtà. Bari, 1965.
Argan, Giulio Carlo. *Progetto e Destino.* Milan, 1965.
"Design," *Edilizia Moderna*, no. 85 (1965).
Dezzi-Bardeschi, M., and L. Vinca-Masini, eds. *Prima Triennale Itinerante d'Architettura Italiana Contemporanea.* Florence, 1965.
Rossi, A. *L'Architettura della Città.* Padua, 1965.
Gregotti, Vittorio. *Il Territorio dell'Architettura.* Milan, 1966.
Cerasi, M. Munir. *Michelucci.* Rome, 1968.
König, Giovanni Klaus. *L'Architettura in Toscana, 1931–1968.* Turin, 1968.
Quaroni, Ludovico. *La Torre di Babele.* Padua, 1968.

INDEX

Sources of Illustrations

Where possible, all sources have been identified.

1. Courtesy Vittorio Gregotti, Milan
2–4. Ugo Mulas, Milan.
5–6. Foto Heliograph, Como.
7. Foto Crimella, Milan.
8. Foto Carla De Benedetti.
9. Foto F. Barsotti, Florence.
10. Courtesy Franco Albini, Milan.
11. Courtesy Marcello Nizzoli.
12. Foto Figini, Milan.
13–14. Foto Heliograph, Como.
15–16. Foto Vasari, Rome.
17. Courtesy Ludovico Quaroni.
18. Courtesy Vittorio Gregotti, Milan.
19. Vittorio Gregotti, Milan.
20. Courtesy B.B.P.R., Milan.
22. Courtesy B.B.P.R., Milan.
23. Courtesy Vittorio Gregotti, Milan.
24. Courtesy Gio Ponti.
25–26. Ugo Mulas, Milan.
27. Fotocielo, Rome.
29. Courtesy B.B.P.R., Milan.
30. Courtesy Vittorio Gregotti, Milan.
31. Foto Villani, Bologna.
32–33. Foto Vasari, Rome.
34. Courtesy Ludovico Quaroni.
35–37. *Casabella*, Milan.
38. Foto Vasari, Rome.
39. *Casabella*, Milan.
40. Casabella (Foto Moisio, Turin).
41. Casabella (Interfoto, Venice).
42. Foto Montacchini, Parma.
43. Foto Casali, Milan.
44. Foto Moncalvo, Turin.
45. *Casabella*, Milan.
46. Foto F. Barsotti, Florence.
47. Photo Lux, Turin.
48. *Casabella*, Milan.
49. *Casabella* (Foto "Fotogramma," Milan).
50. *Casabella* (Foto Oscar Savio, Rome).
51. Courtesy B.P.R., Milan.
52. *Casabella*, Milan.
53. Foto Cresta, Genoa.
54. Foto Oscar Savio, Rome.
55. Foto Dino Sala, Milan.

56. Courtesy Angelo Mangiarotti, Milan.
57. Foto Casali, Milan.
58. Publifoto, Genoa.
59. Foto G. Chiolini, Pavia.
60. Foto Moncalvo, Turin.
61. *Casabella*, Milan.
62. Montecatini Edison.
63. Ugo Mulas, Milan.
64. *Casabella*, Milan.
65. R.M. Fotografia, Milan.
66. Aldo Ballo, Milan.
67. Foto Casali, Milan.
68. Courtesy Vittoriano Viganò, Milan.
69. Attualfoto, Milan.
70. *Casabella*, Milan.
71. Courtesy Ludovico Quaroni.
72. *Casabella*, Milan.
73. Courtesy Ludovico Quaroni.
74. Courtesy Achilli, Canella, D'Angiolini, and Vercelloni, Milan.
75. *Casabella*, Milan.
77. Courtesy Gino Valle (Foto Fulvio Roiter, Udine).
78. Foto Casali, Milan.
79. Foto Oscar Savio, Rome.
80. Ugo Mulas, Milan.
81. Bassechi-Foto, Florence.
82. *Edilizia Moderna.*
83. Ezio Frea, Milan.
85–86. Aldo Ballo, Milan.
87. Foto Studio S. Cavallo, M. Turin.
88. Ghiringhelli Baviera Studio, Milan.
89. Aldo Ballo, Milan.
90. Courtesy A. and P.G. Castiglioni, Milan.
91. Courtesy Quattroruote, Milan.
92. A. Stile Industria.
93. Foto Bombelli.
94. Carrozzeria Pinin Farina, Turin.
95. I.S.O., Milan.
96. Courtesy Marco Zanuso.
97. Foto Fulvio Roiter, Udine.
98. Foto Casali, Milan.
99. Courtesy Silvano Zorzi.
100. Colore Industriale, Milan.
101–102. Facoltà Architettura, Rome.
103–104. *Edilizia Moderna.*
106. Courtesy Vittorio Gregotti, Milan.
107. *Casabella*, Milan (Bazzechi-Foto, Florence).
108–109. Courtesy Ludovico Quaroni.
110. Courtesy Franco Albini and Franca Helg, Milan.